Learn CakePHP

With Unit Testing

Second Edition

Rādhārādhya Dāsa

Apress®

Learn CakePHP: With Unit Testing, Second Edition

Sándor Gömöri
Somogyvamos, Hungary

ISBN-13 (pbk): 978-1-4842-1213-4   ISBN-13 (electronic): 978-1-4842-1212-7
DOI 10.1007/978-1-4842-1212-7

Library of Congress Control Number: 2016949500

Managing Director: Welmoed Spahr
Lead Editor: Steve Anglin
Technical Reviewer: Massimo Nardone
Editorial Board: Steve Anglin, Pramila Balan, Louise Corrigan, Jonathan Gennick,
    Robert Hutchinson, Celestin Suresh John, James Markham, Susan McDermott,
    Matthew Moodie, Ben Renow-Clarke, Gwenan Spearing
Coordinating Editor: Mark Powers
Copy Editor: Michael G. Laraque
Compositor: SPi Global
Indexer: SPi Global
Artist: SPi Global

Distributed to the book trade worldwide by Springer Science+Business Media New York, 233 Spring Street, 6th Floor, New York, NY 10013. Phone 1-800-SPRINGER, fax (201) 348-4505, e-mail orders-ny@springer-sbm.com, or visit www.springeronline.com. Apress Media, LLC is a California LLC and the sole member (owner) is Springer Science+Business Media Finance Inc (SSBM Finance Inc). SSBM Finance Inc is a Delaware corporation.

For information on translations, please e-mail rights@apress.com, or visit www.apress.com.

Apress and friends of ED books may be purchased in bulk for academic, corporate, or promotional use. eBook versions and licenses are also available for most titles. For more information, reference our Special Bulk Sales–eBook Licensing web page at www.apress.com/bulk-sales.

Any source code or other supplementary materials referenced by the author in this text is available to readers at www.apress.com/9781484212134. For detailed information about how to locate your book's source code, go to www.apress.com/source-code/. Readers can also access source code at SpringerLink in the Supplementary Material section for each chapter.

Printed on acid-free paper

Call out Gouranga and be happy

Contents at a Glance

About the Author xv

About the Technical Reviewer xvii

Acknowledgments xix

Introduction xxi

About the Book xxiii

■Chapter 1: What Is CakePHP? 3

■Chapter 2: What Is Unit Testing? 9

■Chapter 3: Clean Code 15

■Chapter 4: Test-Driven Development 19

■Chapter 5: Development Cycle 23

■Chapter 6: Preparing for Testing 29

■Chapter 7: Fixtures 49

■Chapter 8: Model Tests 59

■Chapter 9: Controller Tests 1 67

■Chapter 10: Mocks 81

■Chapter 11: Controller Tests 2 89

■Chapter 12: Test Suites 95

■**Chapter 13: Testing from Command Line** **99**

■**Chapter 14: Goodies** **105**

■**Appendix A: References by Chapter** **111**

Index **113**

Contents

About the Author xv

About the Technical Reviewer xvii

Acknowledgments xix

Introduction xxi

About the Book xxiii

■Chapter 1: What Is CakePHP? 3

    Main Features 3

        Short Learning Curve 4

        Convention over Configuration 4

        Easy Installation 4

        MIT Licensing 4

        Automatic Code Generation 4

        Built-in Validation 5

        MVC Architecture 5

        Clean URLs and Routes 5

        Flexible Caching 5

        Built-in Localization 5

        Integrated Unit Testing 6

        And More 6

    Summary 6

▓Chapter 2: What Is Unit Testing? 9

From Manual Testing to Unit Tests 9

Arguments... 9

Argument #1: It's Impossible to Test All Variations 10

Argument #2: Writing Tests Takes Too Much Time................................... 10

Argument #3: Writing Tests Is Hard 10

Argument #4: I Don't Need Tests; I Know My Code.................................. 10

Argument #5: It Is Just a Waste of Time 10

Argument #6: The Tests Might Have Their Own Bugs 11

Argument #7: Development Breaks Tests... 11

Why Should We Write Tests? 11

Test Functionality... 11

Refactoring 12

Getting Fast Feedback... 12

Quality Code 12

Use the Best of Your Brain 12

Save Time and Money.. 13

Summary... 13

▓Chapter 3: Clean Code 15

How to Write Clean Code... 15

Comments 15

Naming 16

Methods.. 16

Code Formatting 16

MVC 16

How Tests Help in Writing Clean Code...17

    Planning...17

    Refactoring..17

Summary...17

■Chapter 4: Test-Driven Development...19

PHP TDD Tools...19

    PHPUnit...19

    Codeception..19

    SimpleTest..19

    Atoum...20

    Selenium...20

TDD Development Cycle...20

    Step #1: Write Test...20

    Step #2: Write Code...20

    Step #3: Refactor...20

    Step #4: Test Again..21

    Step #5: Write Code for New Features..21

Summary...21

■Chapter 5: Development Cycle..23

Agile...23

    The Agile Manifesto..23

    12 Principles Behind the Manifesto...24

    How CakePHP Supports Agile Development......................................24

The Agile Roadmap to Value..25

    Product Vision...25

    Product Roadmap...25

    Release Plan...25

    Sprint Planning...25

Daily Meetings 25

Sprint Review 26

Sprint Retrospective 26

Summary 26

■Chapter 6: Preparing for Testing 29

Installing 29

Install Webserver 29

Install MySQL 30

Install PHP 30

Post Installation 31

Install Composer 32

Install CakePHP 32

Installing PHPUnit 33

Install phpMyAdmin 34

Check Your Test Setup 34

Preparing 35

Set Debug Level 35

Set Up Test Database 35

Set Up Session Handling 42

Create the Default Layout 42

CakePHP Models 42

CakePHP Controllers 44

CakePHP Views 44

Baking 44

Clean It Up 46

Let's Play 46

Summary 47

■**Chapter 7: Fixtures** **49**

Creating Fixtures 49

On the Fly 49

Importing the Existing Model Schema 53

Loading Fixtures into Your Tests 55

Summary 57

■**Chapter 8: Model Tests** **59**

Names of Test Functions 61

Assertions 61

Fail First 61

Passing Test 62

Tests and Fat Models 63

Test Callbacks 63

Summary 64

■**Chapter 9: Controller Tests 1** **67**

Overview of the Baked Controller 67

The Magic Behind Bake 72

Creating Controller Tests 72

About Integration Tests 76

Assertion Methods 76

Setting Request Data 77

Summary 78

■**Chapter 10: Mocks** **81**

Mocking Sessions 81

Mocking Model Methods 82

Expects Method 83

A More Complex Mock Example 84

Mocking Core PHP Functions 85

Summary 87

■Chapter 11: Controller Tests 2 89

Testing with Authentication 89

Testing JSON Response 91

Summary 93

■Chapter 12: Test Suites 95

Using TestSuite 95

Using phpunit.xml 96

Summary 96

■Chapter 13: Testing from Command Line 99

Debug Messages 99

Run All Tests 99

Run Test Suites 99

Run All Tests in a File 100

Filtering Test Cases 100

Understanding a Failing Test's Output 100

Interrupting Tests 103

Summary 103

■Chapter 14: Goodies 105

Code Coverage 105

Fixtures Data 107

Testing Private Methods 107

Testing Views 108

Testing Components 108

Testing Helpers 109

Testing Plugins 110

Summary 110

Appendix A: References by Chapter 111

What Is Unit Testing? 111

Clean Code 111

Test-Driven Development 111

Development Cycle 112

Others 112

Index 113

About the Author

Rādhārādhya Dāsa started to code for the Web in plain HTML while in college in 1998. As the Web evolved, he turned to PHP, then to JavaScript. With the advent of mobile technologies, he began to experiment with Java for Android development.

He's a big fan of CakePHP and jQuery frameworks, open source, and pizza, all of which are essential in his web development.

About the Technical Reviewer

Massimo Nardone holds a master of science degree in computer science from the University of Salerno, Italy. He has worked as a project manager, software engineer, research engineer, chief security architect, information security manager, PCI/SCADA auditor, and senior lead IT security/cloud/SCADA architect for many years. He currently works as chief information security office (CISO) for Cargotec Oyj. He has more than 22 years of work experience in IT, including security, SCADA, cloud computing, IT infrastructure, mobile, security, and World Wide Web technology areas for both national and international projects. He worked as a visiting lecturer and supervisor for exercises at the Networking Laboratory of the Helsinki University of Technology (Aalto University). He has been programming and teaching how to program with Android, Perl, PHP, Java, VB, Python, C/C++, and MySQL for more than 20 years. He holds four international patents (PKI, SIP, SAML, and Proxy areas) and is the coauthor of *Pro Android Games* (Apress, 2015).

Acknowledgments

I would like to thank you for spending your time reading this book.

I also should say thank you to the core CakePHP team and everybody else who's contributed anything, small or big, to this wonderful framework.

Finally, special thanks go to Italy for pizza and to Hungary for Túró Rudi—both are essential for web development.

Introduction

I love to code for the Web, but I don't like hunting for bugs I've made myself. And I hate—I mean really hate—hunting for bugs made by other people.

Most of the time, our code depends on other people. We use frameworks, utilities, and objects created and maintained by others. All thid-party code falls into this category. As web developers, all of us upgrade our code to implement new features, to fix bugs, or to make our creations compatible with new server versions. Any upgrades could introduce new behaviors, new interfaces, and certainly new bugs. Whether you work alone or as a member of a team, we all depend on one another's code.

Writing code is not like writing a letter to grandma. Actually, writing code is not writing at all. If we spend enough time planning, and if the requirements are clear and don't change during development, writing code could be something like writing a letter. But in reality it's something else. When we write code, we first write one small part, then check it, modify it, check it again, write something else connected to the first part, check that also, check the first part again, and, when it fails, modify it again, check it again, and on and on. Sound familiar?

Do you repeatedly push the Refresh button of your favorite browser to check the output, just because you wrote two lines of code? Are you bored of filling the same form a hundred times with different inputs to check how it will be processed on the server side? Are `var_dump` and `debug()` your best friends? Does everything work fine in development but after installation nothing happens? Or worse, are there just a few things not working in the production environment, but you have no idea why not? Or maybe you just want to learn a new approach that will give you better, simpler, and more maintainable code. Maybe you're looking for something that will help you identify bugs and save time. If so, keep reading.

About the Book

I wrote this book for the following audiences: people who have programming skills and want to improve the quality of their code, people who have heard about unit testing but are still not clear what it is or how it works, people who love CakePHP and want to take advantage of what it offers, and people who have spent a lot of time searching for bugs after a third-party upgrade.

The examples in this book use CakePHP, but the first half of the book is not framework- or language-specific. I hope unit testing and the ideas presented in this book will help you as much as they've helped me.

Why I Wrote This Book

I started to use CakePHP at version 1.1. The framework is wonderful and improving nicely, with an open and helpful staff and community. It helped me to became a better programmer.

When I started to code, I did everything from scratch. I did not know about programming patterns, utilities, or libraries. I was able to build middle-size systems this way.

After a while, I decided that mixing application logic and presentation logic have more cons than pros, so I started to use Smarty (http://smarty.net/). Smarty was a great help. In time, it helped me to see that my best practices were really my worst practices. I knew I needed something more.

I realized there are a few features I need in most of my web applications. I started to think about how I code and, after some time, came up with an extremely simple and dull framework, without really knowing that frameworks exist.

That was when I heard about MVC (Model-View-Controller) Pattern. At first, it seemed like an unnecessary complication in the code, but I wanted to give it a try anyway. When I tried to understand MVC, I found some information about frameworks. I tried CodeIgniter (http://ellislab.com/codeigniter), and then CakePHP (http://cakephp.org).

The first bite of CakePHP was awful, especially because I was (and am) a big fan of bake auto-code generation. I thought that the whole framework just saved so much time and produced a much clearer and more maintainable code.

But eventually, I would use CakePHP to write an online accounting system. It was about money, so the code should always work as expected. I spent a lot of time testing—by clicking links, filling out forms, typing in test data again and again—trying to understand why the code failed when it failed. But that was OK. That's how you make things work.

CakePHP version 1.3 came out, and then Cake 2. I wanted to upgrade, but upgrading seemed like such a hassle. I was reluctant. I didn't know how much time I should spend upgrading, or how many hidden bugs would be in the code. Relying on error messages when the base framework of a third-party code changes is a nightmare.

I had heard about unit testing, but I actually didn't care. A code that'll test my code? Silly. But I tried to understand, and I found many articles in support of unit testing. You can read them for yourself under "Arguments" in Chapter 2. Finally, I gave them a try, and they helped. They helped a lot.

I think many of you have had similar experiences. Let's try to shorten our learning curve.

I hope this book will help you, and that my suggestions can save you some time.

My Development Environment

I tried to use code examples that are independent of the environment, but, as we all know, this is impossible. With that in mind, following is my system and the software I'm using:

- Ubuntu 16.04
- PHP 7.0.4
- CakePHP 3.2.8
- PHPUnit 5.3.2
- MySQL 5.0.12
- MySQL Workbench 6.3.4
- PHPStorm 10
- xdebug 2.4.0

Who This Book Is For

This book is for novice and intermediate programmers. It assumes that you have a general understanding of PHP and object-oriented programming (OOP).

It's good if you are familiar with CakePHP, especially in later chapters. But even if you're not, you will probably still be able to understand most of the principles and codes.

Secrets of the cake industry

CHAPTER 1

What Is CakePHP?

PHPs market share for web sites is more than 80%.[1] Why is it so popular? It's easy and fast to learn, available on nearly every web server, and used for popular applications. It has a lot of wonderful frameworks, such as Zend,[2] Symfony,[3] and, perhaps our favorite, CakePHP.

The frameworks are different in their approach, complexity, and style. I think CakePHP stands out, with its short learning curve, concentrating on rapid development.

Frameworks help you to speed up your development, give you well-organized, maintainable, and reusable code, and assets for handling security, localization, and more.

The CakePHP manual[4] (or "cookbook") states: "CakePHP is a free[5], open-source[6], rapid-development[7] framework[8] for PHP[9]."

I think CakePHP is most famous for its ten-minute blog tutorial. And, yes, it's true: with CakePHP, you *can* build a working blog in ten minutes! And you can build bigger web applications just as fast, without sacrificing flexibility.

Main Features

Most popular PHP frameworks try to offer solutions to the same problems. So, choosing one is not easy. Most developers work with one framework and know a bit about a few others. And certainly, everybody thinks the best is what they use. So, in the following sections, let's see why I choose CakePHP.

Electronic supplementary material The online version of this chapter (doi:10.1007/978-1-4842-1212-7_1) contains supplementary material, which is available to authorized users.

---

[1]W[3] (Web Technology Surveys), "Usage statistics and market share for PHP websites," https://w3techs.com/technologies/details/pl-php/all/all, 2009–2016.
[2]http://framework.zend.com/
[3]https://symfony.com/
[4]http://book.cakephp.org
[5]http://en.wikipedia.org/wiki/MIT_License
[6]http://en.wikipedia.org/wiki/Open_source
[7]http://en.wikipedia.org/wiki/Rapid_application_development
[8]http://en.wikipedia.org/wiki/Application_framework
[9]http://www.php.net/

© Sándor Gömöri 2016
S. Gömöri, *Learn CakePHP*, DOI 10.1007/978-1-4842-1212-7_1

Short Learning Curve

CakePHP's learning curve is short. You can become familiar with the main API methods in a week and gain deep insight in a month. CakePHP 3 represents a significant change, and I think it makes the learning curve even shorter.

Convention over Configuration

If you follow CakePHP's conventions practically, you do not have to configure anything at all, thanks to the framework's idea of "convention over configuration." Cake's conventions are simple to follow and learn.

Controller class names are plural, CamelCased, and end in "Controller." So the Post's controller will be `PostsController`. It will be in the `/src/PostsController.php` file. It's corresponding model file will be at `/src/Model/Table/PostsTable.php`, which will be linked to the posts table in our database. Its view files will be in the `/src/Template/Posts` folder.

Table class names are plural and CamelCased; table names corresponding to CakePHP models are plural and underscored in English.

View template files are named after the controller functions they display, in an underscored form, and they are automatically mapped from URLs.

If you cannot (or, in some rare case, you do not want) to follow conventions, you can easily configure everything.

Easy Installation

You will see how to install CakePHP in Chapter 6. Actually, with one line of code, you can download and install CakePHP. So, installation takes about two seconds or less.

MIT Licensing[10]

The MIT (Massachusetts Institute of Technology) License is a free software license. It permits reuse of the code within proprietary and free software also. The MIT License is also compatible with many copyleft licenses, such as GPL.

Ruby on Rails, Node.js, jQuery, and many other frameworks are permissible under the MIT License.

Automatic Code Generation

CakePHP has a built-in console shell called bake, by which we can generate a basic model, controller, and view files. I think it is one of the best tools in rapid development. By using bake, you can start to have a working skeleton in a very early phase of your

---

[10]http://en.wikipedia.org/wiki/MIT_License

development. If you follow Cake's conventions, bake will detect your database tables and fields and, based on this, will generate code for you—always a good start. You will see automatic code generation in action in Chapter 6.

Built-in Validation[11]

Validating input data is very important. Validation ensures that an application operates on clean, correct, and useful data. It means that validation can check data from the security viewpoint—check if it is acceptable, such as if it is within a certain range, in the right format, and more.

Models generated by bake have validation rules, and they are a good starting point from which to become familiar with validation.

MVC[12] Architecture

Perhaps MVC (Model-View-Controller) architecture is not an extraordinary feature of CakePHP, as almost all PHP frameworks follow the same pattern. But as a paradigm, a way of thinking, it still will help you to create better code.

Clean URLs and Routes

Cake helps you to create simple, clean URLs and practically gives you 100% freedom in manipulating your web application's URLs. By default, URLs are built up like this: /controller/method/parameter, so `posts/edit/1` will be mapped to `PostsController`'s edit method, and it will get 1 as its only parameter.

Flexible Caching[13]

CakePHP has six different caching engines built in, such as FileCache, Memcached, Redis, and others. You can change caching engines any time smoothly, as they have the same interface. If you want something really special, you can add your own caching system.

Built-in Localization

Localization and internationalization can be either a nightmare or something really simple. Cake provides a really good way to have both without much effort. You just have to create your translation files in `gettext` format and use the `__()` method when you want to print out something to the screen.

---

[11]http://en.wikipedia.org/wiki/Data_validation
[12]http://en.wikipedia.org/wiki/Model-view-controller
[13]http://en.wikipedia.org/wiki/Web_cache

Integrated Unit Testing

Perhaps for us, the most important aspect of CakePHP is that it has an integrated unit testing system. It uses PHPUnit and gives us a few really useful classes and methods for testing.

And More

CakePHP also has an active, friendly, and helpful developer team[14] and community. Community is very important when you get stuck. The CakePHP community fields tens of thousands of questions on stack overflow related to CakePHP, has an active Google mailing group and Google + group, and an online forum.[15]

CakePHP is one of most famous PHP frameworks used by thousands of web sites and applications and beloved and frequently used by many developers around the world.

CakePHP makes building web applications simpler, faster, and easier.

Summary

In this chapter, you learned about PHP frameworks generally and then took a closer look at CakePHP and its main features. I went through the main conventions of the framework, by which we can avoid any configuration issues. From among Cake's main features, I emphasized automatic code generation (and, perhaps, integrated unit testing), as this is the main topic of this book.

---

[14]http://cakephp.lighthouseapp.com/contributors
[15]http://discourse.cakephp.org/

Give me your hand, baby

What Is Unit Testing?

Unit testing allows you to test your software in isolation. Normally, unit tests are small, fast, and test just a short piece of code—a unit—such as a function. A unit test is code designed to test other code.

It helps to keep the code short, easy to understand, and easy to read. It helps, too, to write more maintainable code. As a result, this helps to create software with fewer bugs. Unit tests automatize the testing process.

Unit tests alone will not guarantee perfect, bug-free applications, but they help a lot.

From Manual Testing to Unit Tests

When you write code, you have to be sure that it will do its job. As I am discussing testing PHP, beginners should test in the browser. Write the code; open the browser; give different inputs; and check if the output is what is wanted. Sound familiar? This is called *manual testing*, and with this, we test functionality, not our code.

The next step is to have a system to automatize testing, so that you do not have to manually click here and there in the browser in order to check your software. There are many tools with which to do this. The two main approaches are test-driven development (TDD) and behavior-driven development (BDD).

TDD, in short, starts with writing tests *before* you write your code. This approach relies on unit tests.

As unit tests are for small pieces of code, they are easy to write, and your code is easily covered by them.

In BDD, tests of any unit should be specified in terms of the desired behavior of the unit.

Arguments

There are common arguments against writing unit tests. I want to highlight the advantages of unit testing, by addressing those arguments and sharing my own experience with the issues those arguments address. Then, you can try out unit testing for yourself and make your own decision.

© Sándor Gömöri 2016
S. Gömöri, *Learn CakePHP*, DOI 10.1007/978-1-4842-1212-7_2

Argument #1: It's Impossible to Test All Variations

Yes, it's true. You will not be able to test all possible variations. But at least a unit test will show what variations are covered by your tests. If you can determine that the application fails because of a variation not covered by the unit test, you just extend the test.

For example, if I had a test that runs successfully with positive integers, I could extend the test later for 0, negative integers, or floats, when necessary.

Argument #2: Writing Tests Takes Too Much Time

Writing—and maintaining—extra code takes time. That's obvious. But writing is itself just one of many time-consuming factors. What are the others? Time spent trying to understand our own code three or four months after writing it, or time spent trying to understand someone else's code. Time spent trying to find the particular piece of code with the bug. Time spent reviewing our code whenever third-party code is changed. When we add up the time spent on all these things, it starts to look like unit testing *could* save time. Saving time means saving money, but be careful. Unit tests *could* save time; it's not that they definitely *will* save time. You have to use the tests correctly.

Learning to use unit tests takes time too. But I think the learning curve is short, and there will be a return, even the very first time you use them.

Argument #3: Writing Tests Is Hard

Writing tests is easy. Writing *good* tests is hard. But it just takes a little practice.

There is an exception. Writing tests for spaghetti code, or for functions that do many things, is hard. So, when you run into difficult tests, you should make sure that this is an indication that your code requires refactoring.

Argument #4: I Don't Need Tests; I Know My Code

Nearly 99.9% of the time, you do not code alone. We frequently use third-party code. And we tend to forget, or to change, the way we think about coding, as time passes. Maybe it seemed clear when we first wrote the code, but after a while, we may have to spend minutes (or hours) to understand what we did.

Many times, I write tests for my helper functions consisting of five or six lines. These functions are much simpler to test when your code sits on different servers, different PHP versions. It is simpler to test different inputs—even with data that should not be there at all—such as division by zero.

Argument #5: It Is Just a Waste of Time

This argument is given by web developers who start to write unit tests and have argument #4 in mind. They often say, "I created some unit tests, but when running, they did not find any bugs at all. I think it was a waste of time."

OK, now you have tests. So, you have an asset in hand that can help you to check the same parts of your code after you make some changes or do some refactoring. At least, for this, you do not have to go back to manual testing any more. Write more tests, go back to your code after three months, and check the difference. Writing some code and maintaining it is two different things. With unit tests, you will not waste as much time on maintaining the code as without them.

Argument #6: The Tests Might Have Their Own Bugs

Yes. Any code might have bugs. But unit tests are short, so it's easy to write them bug-free. It's entirely possible to write tests that pass even when they should fail. Once again, the solution is practice.

Never forget: Tests show the presence of errors, not the absence of errors.

Argument #7: Development Breaks Tests

As you add layers to your development cycle, you should maintain your tests as well. When the code changes, the corresponding tests should also change; otherwise, the tests will fail. But, if you change the code, you'll know how to change the test.

Actually, this is one of the advantages to having tests. When I refactor my code, the test should run successfully. If I change the signature or return value of the code, the test will fail, or it may run successfully. If it fails, you will see where it can create problems or bugs in the code. So, it promotes safe changes.

Why Should We Write Tests?

Tests significantly shorten testing time, which eventually saves money. Tests help in writing quality code and are essential assets in refactoring. They will change the way you think about code.

Test Functionality

When we first write a code, we should check that it really does what we want. We all do this—with or without unit tests. Actually, var_dump and its friends are also tests. They just don't fulfill the real purpose of tests.

After some time, you will definitely have to implement changes in old code, either because of bugs or just because you want to streamline what you've done. In that case, too, you'll need something to test whether the code still does what you want. Manual testing is boring, slow, and ineffective.

Manual testing is much more time-consuming than any other testing system, at least if you do it prudently. The same method can be invoked at many places in your application, and you should test everywhere, to make sure your application is working as expected. On top of that, you should have a list of possible inputs, such as "I should test it with negative numbers, zero, letters, special characters." And perhaps you've neglected to test everything before you deploy to production. No, that never happens!

Refactoring

Renaming variables or functions increases readability of code. But you should take care that renaming does not introduce new bugs or conflicts. The same is true for changing a method's signature or return values. Tests are there to help you.

Sometimes, there are pieces of code that actually don't have any connection to the goal of the code or that don't do anything at all. Obviously, you want to remove such code, but then you'd have to check that the bulk of the code still works. You can remove unwanted code snippets safely, if your code is covered by tests, as the tests will fail if you have removed something useful.

At other times, you may know that your code is wrong but don't want to spend the time to fix it. So, you just leave a comment in the code, such as `// TODO: it will break if $num = 0`. A failing test is much, much more clean.

There is a famous saying: "If it ain't broke, don't fix it." My hard-written code is working, what are you talking about? you may ask. Simply put, however, the saying is not true for software development. Refactoring is a very important part of development. By successfully refactoring your code, you will end up with the same results as you would without doing so, but your code will be reusable, maintainable, faster, cleaner, and better if you do.

Getting Fast Feedback

Fast feedback is important. Developers don't have the time to click every link, push every button in every possible order, push the browser's Back button multiple times, fill out forms with a variety of data (even with malicious data), or deploy new code and wait for clients' feedback.

I think Firebug (`https://getfirebug.com`) is a good example. I open the HTML tab and change something, and *immediately* I'll see the result in the browser.

There are other tools, for other languages, that give immediate feedback by actually running tests after every semicolon or file save. These are extremely powerful development tools. They are not available in PHP, but, regardless, tests are the best tools for this.

Quality Code

Tests run in isolation. So, by running a test, you are verifying a particular piece of code that does not depend on other pieces. But it is easy to violate the *single responsibility* principle. Tests add another viewpoint to our code-writing process. More on this can be found in Chapter 3.

Use the Best of Your Brain

Under pressure, even the most clever people (yes, even programmers) make stupid mistakes.

Have you ever written something like `if(3 < 5)`? Never? You will, I promise. There is a good chance you might break something even with the most trivial code or code change. Are you always relaxed? Do you always have more than enough time to write your code? Is your boss always happy? Are your clients always patient? Do you always have a clear specification? Do your kids sleep all night? If not, you'll make stupid mistakes. Tests help you to check your code in an easy way.

Save Time and Money

As I already mentioned, one way or another, you'll test your code. But you can choose a way that is more effective. You can choose a way that will let you spend less time fixing bugs and refactoring and more time actually writing code. Saving time is fun—you can always spend that time watching the next episode of your favorite TV show—and saving time saves money.

Summary

In this chapter, you learned why we test, what unit testing is, and what the arguments against it are. From this, you learned that you can save time on maintaining code—as it can be as foreign after a few months as if it were written by someone else—and how tests help you to use the best of your brain.

Our APIs seem to have some communication problems

CHAPTER 3

■ ■ ■

Clean Code

Who cares about the code? If it runs, then it's fine. Right? I don't think so.

There are several reasons why you should care about code quality.

First, the quality of your code will determine the quality of the software. If you think you can have great software with messy code, you're dreaming. Second, clean code saves time. You will spend more time *reading* your code more than you spend *writing* it. The other people in your team will also spend a good part of their time reading your code. And you will spend time reading other people's code too. Clean code is easy to read, so clean code saves time. Third, your code is a reflection of yourself. If you don't value quality in your code, you won't get hired. Messy code means you don't hold yourself, or your work, to a very high standard. Clients and employers demand quality.

Clean code is maintainable. It is easy to read and easy to understand. That means it's easy to use and easy to change. Clean code is straightforward.

How to Write Clean Code

Clean code doesn't require loads of time. Writing clean code is a habit that requires some attention during writing and refactoring. Luckily, it's a habit you can learn.

Never forget: We write code for machines and for people. People are more important.

Here are a few hints for how to write clean code. When you work in a team you should fix at least these options.

Comments

There are people who say that unit testing can be a substitute for comments. There are others who say "don't comment—refactor." Both approaches have their merits, but comments can be a great help to write better code.

To learn when and what to comment takes time. I think the best approach is to view comments as Post-its in our code. So if something is not straightforward or takes some time to understand, comment it. For example, most of the time, I comment regular expressions. But don't forget: you should update your comments on code change. Otherwise, you can run into misleading or confusing comments.

© Sándor Gömöri 2016
S. Gömöri, *Learn CakePHP*, DOI 10.1007/978-1-4842-1212-7_3

Using PHPDoc (www.phpdoc.org/) is a best practice and is used by CakePHP's core. PHPDoc makes it possible to generate documentation directly from your source code. It promotes standardized comments for all your classes and methods.

Naming

We should name our classes, methods, variables, parameters, etc. Names should be descriptive and meaningful. "Foo" and "bar" work well in short code examples but can be very confusing in production code.

When you are totally immersed in your code, a variable named $lld may be clear, but wouldn't $last_login_date be a little bit more readable and easier to understand?

By its conventions, CakePHP uses underscored names for database tables, field names, and view files. For class names, it uses CamelCased names. For variable and parameter names, you can choose any of these; however, just stick to one. So, if you prefer underscored variable names, underscore all of your variable names, and do not mix in CamelCased names.

It is best to follow the PHP Standards Recommendations (PSR) (www.php-fig.org/psr). PSR-1 recommends using CamelCased method names. Using verbs for method names is a best practice.

Methods

Methods should do one, and only one, thing and do it well. This is the single responsibility principle. This means that methods should be short, which means that they will be easy to understand. There are developers who recommend a maximum of three lines of code.

If a function accepts more than two arguments, it is a good candidate for refactoring.

CakePHP's ORM is a good example of using method chaining. It can significantly improve the readability of your code, or it can significantly mess it up. So, please learn from the good examples.

Code Formatting

Historians say the bloodiest battle in history was that of Stalingrad, in 1942. They say this because they never attended a meeting at which developers try to agree on the code style that they are going to follow in a new project.

Thanks to PSR-2, the battle is over, and we have a recommendation to follow.

Code formatting covers indentation, where to place opening and closing brackets, where to put new lines, and more.

MVC

As MVC (Model-View–Controller) stresses, do not mix model, controller, and view functionality in the same files or classes. This also helps to keep your code clean.

Perhaps there are a lot of other things that you can do to ensure clean code, but to list and introduce all the options here is beyond the scope of this book. You can use clever tools, such as PHP Mess Detector (https://phpmd.org/), to help you to write clean code.

How Tests Help in Writing Clean Code

Even if you use unit tests in your applications, you can still end up with messy code. Unit testing won't do the work for you. I'll cover this topic in more detail in Chapter 4.

Planning

Planning is a very important part of creating great software, but people like me and you are often too impatient to plan everything down to the last detail. We like to get our hands dirty as soon as possible. Unfortunately, this kind of coding creates problems. Using unit tests encourages us to think things over (or plan) during development. If I want to add a new feature to a web application, I'll certainly think about how it will function. Without at least this much planning, I won't be able to write the code. When it runs, I'm finished—at least until someone detects a bug. When I write a test, I have to think about the possible and acceptable inputs, the output, and the return value. Writing tests helps us to think from a distance, on a more abstract level, and test-driven development (TDD) helps us to get the best out of it.

Refactoring

As long as your test doesn't fail, you can be sure the code you've tested does what it should. Tests help to check if changes in the code have broken anything. Because unit tests run in isolation, they help to produce better, simpler code.

With tests, you do not have to worry about changing a function's signature or return values' type. Tests will show where you have to apply changes for function calls.

If your tests are not just a few lines, this may be a sign of a broken single responsibility principle in your code. This is often true if you change your test after refactoring your code. Remember this, and you will end up with cleaner code.

Summary

In this chapter, I introduced the idea and importance of clean code. You learned a few principles to follow to ensure clean code and why naming or code formatting matters. Finally, you saw how unit tests can help in writing cleaner code.

Let's start to play by trying and doing

CHAPTER 4

Test-Driven Development

Developers who depend heavily on unit tests use a technique known as "test-driven development," or TDD.

TDD is a software development process whereby you write tests before you implement code. So, the tests guide the developer to write the code itself. TDD is a cyclical process, with 4+1 steps: write tests, write code, refactor, test again, and repeat the process again.

PHP TDD Tools

There are many tools that can be of great help in TDD with PHP.

PHPUnit

PHPUnit (https://phpunit.de/) is the de facto standard tool for unit testing and TDD for PHP. It is integrated into Cake, so you will become familiar with using it soon.

There are other tools, however, that also have a growing community and provide support.

Codeception

Codeception (http://codeception.com/) has support for writing unit tests, functional tests, and acceptance tests. It is integrated into a few PHP development frameworks, such as Zend, Symfony, Laravel, and others.

SimpleTest

SimpleTest (http://simpletest.org/) is an easy-to-use framework with SSL, proxies, and authentication support. Users of JUnit will be familiar with its interface.

© Sándor Gömöri 2016
S. Gömöri, *Learn CakePHP*, DOI 10.1007/978-1-4842-1212-7_4

Atoum

Atoum (https://github.com/atoum) is a relatively new player that uses new PHP features introduced in PHP version 5.3.

Selenium

Selenium (http://www.seleniumhq.org/) is actually more comprehensive than the previously mentioned tools, as it is a sophisticated, robust system that automates browsers. With it, a web application as a whole can be tested.

TDD Development Cycle

TDD requires a different way of thinking and a different style of coding. Let's see what it takes. With CakePHP, the subject at hand, you do not have to start from scratch. Its framework already includes a lot of great features. So, now we have to concentrate only on our application development.

Step #1: Write Test

Write a unit test for your nonexistent code. As you write the test—and *before* you actually write any code—consider all the possible inputs, errors, and outputs. This step adds an extra, abstract—but important—layer.

The first time you run your unit test, it will fail. It should fail, because the code you're testing doesn't yet exist.

By the one-test method, you produce one or more assertions based on possible inputs or errors.

Most of the time, I start by writing model tests. I create a test method that calls one of the corresponding model's methods (for example, getUserComments()), even if it does not exist at the moment. I know what to expect as a result, so I make the assertion. That means that I have to decide the type of the value returned by the method.

Step #2: Write Code

Now that you've written the test, you can start writing the code. In this step, I create the model class's getUserComments() method. When I think it is OK, I simply run the test and see if it fails or not.

Your code is ready when all of your tests pass.

While writing code, perhaps it is best to follow the principles described in Chapter 3.

Step #3: Refactor

Once all your tests pass successfully, you can start to refactor your code, cleaning up unnecessary variables, function calls, etc.

This is an important part. While we are considering small code fractions and are in the right mindset to understand their problems and solutions to them, this is the best time to rethink solutions and keep them as simple as possible.

Step #4: Test Again

Now rerun your tests. If one or more tests doesn't pass, you have introduced a new bug during refactoring. If all your tests pass, your code is *probably* OK. But don't forget arguments #1 and #6 from Chapter 2.

Step #5: Write Code for New Features

This step requires that you restart the same process, but with another task. Don't forget to thoroughly test this part too. Changes you've made anywhere in your code could also affect this part and vice versa. This means that working on something can initiate a bug or break a test somewhere else.

Summary

In this chapter, you learned what test-driven development is and how it is connected to unit testing. I listed a few of the main PHP tools that facilitate TDD. Of these, PHPUnit is the most important to us, as it is integrated into CakePHP. I then went through the development cycle of TDD, in CakePHP and in general.

The great cycle of life

CHAPTER 5

Development Cycle

There are quite a few development models. In my opinion, choosing the right one can be an important part of the development process, especially when taste and practice really differ. There are also different ways to work with web and desktop applications. All of us have our favorite practices. Let me share mine with you. It is Agile Software Development.

Agile

Agile Software Development is a set of software development principles whereby requirements and solutions result from team collaboration. It promotes adaptive planning, evolutionary development, early delivery, and continuous improvement, and it encourages rapid and flexible response to change.

The Agile Manifesto (`http://agilemanifesto.org/`) is short and simple.

The Agile Manifesto

"We are uncovering better ways of developing software by doing it and helping others do it. Through this work we have come to value:

1. Individuals and interactions over processes and tools

2. Working software over comprehensive documentation

3. Customer collaboration over contract negotiation

4. Responding to change over following a plan

That is, while there is value in the items on the right, we value the items on the left more."

© Sándor Gömöri 2016
S. Gömöri, *Learn CakePHP*, DOI 10.1007/978-1-4842-1212-7_5

12 Principles Behind the Manifesto

There are 12 principles behind the Agile Manifesto.

1. The highest priority is to satisfy the customer through early and continuous delivery of valuable software.

2. Changing requirements are welcome, even late in development. Agile processes harness change for the customer's competitive advantage.

3. Working software is delivered frequently, from a couple of weeks to a couple of months, with a preference toward the shorter timescale.

4. Businesspeople and developers must work together daily throughout the project.

5. Projects are built by motivated individuals. Give them the environment and support their needs, and trust them to get the job done.

6. The most efficient and effective method of conveying information to and within a development team is face-to-face conversation.

7. Working software is the primary measure of progress.

8. Agile processes promote sustainable development. The sponsors, developers, and users should be able to maintain a constant pace indefinitely.

9. Continuous attention to technical excellence and good design enhances agility.

10. Simplicity—the art of maximizing the amount of work not done—is essential.

11. The best architectures, requirements, and designs emerge from self-organizing teams.

12. At regular intervals, the team reflects on how to become more effective, then tunes and adjusts its behavior accordingly.

How CakePHP Supports Agile Development

As you can see, some of the preceding principles require a particular mindset, a way of thinking, and some of them actually require some technical support.

Baking is a good way to get something viewable in a short time. So it helps to adhere to principles 1, 4, and 7.

Thanks to CakePHP's MVC pattern and the wonderful new ORM introduced in CakePHP3, late changes are easy at least for models. Even in late phases it is easy to handle database table or field changes. So it meets principles 2 and 7.

Regular delivery (principle 3) is more likely a habit or a workflow organization question than a technical matter. Still, because of the two previously mentioned points, Cake gives us some help to achieve this.

TDD helps you to adhere to principles 9 and 10.

The Agile Roadmap to Value

Any project requires some steps or stages. With Agile, it is the Roadmap to Value that provides the high-level overview of the project. The roadmap has seven stages.

Product Vision

At stage 1, the product owner outlines the product vision: a definition of the project, how it will serve the user's (or company's) goals, and who the target users are.

An example: For people who want a simple and easy blog, the cakeBlog is a blog engine that provides minimal features concentrated on blogging. Unlike other engines with too many features, our software is for real dummies.

By my estimate, 90–95% of the time, a customer doesn't really know what he or she wants. He/She has some idea, but it's very far from being specific. That's OK; it's not a problem—remember principle 2.

Product Roadmap

The product owner creates a product roadmap at stage 2. It is a high-level view of the product requirements, with roughly estimated schedules of when these requirements will be developed.

Release Plan

At stage 3, the product owner creates a release plan, what is actually a timetable of releases of working software. It will have many releases, with the highest priority features launching first.

Sprint Planning

Sprints are iterations in which the software is created. At stage 4, the team plan sprints. Sprint planning happens at the start of each sprint, where the team decides what requirements should be included in this sprint.

Daily Meetings

During each sprint, the team has daily meetings. This is stage 5. The meetings are no more than 15 minutes and concern what was completed yesterday, what will be worked on today, and any potential roadblocks.

Sprint Review

At the end of every sprint, the working product created during the sprint is shown. This is stage 6.

Sprint Retrospective

At the end of each sprint retrospective—stage 7—is a meeting during which the team discusses how the sprint went and ideas for improvements in the next sprint.

Summary

In this chapter, I covered Agile Software Development principles and phases. You learned how CakePHP supports Agile development. Even if you follow other development methods, CakePHP offers you useful tools for them also.

Bill felt his training was not complete

CHAPTER 6

Preparing for Testing

Installing

To have everything up and running, you have to install a web server, MySQL server, PHP, CakePHP (http://book.cakephp.org), and PHPUnit (http://phpunit.de). I will go through all these procedures, using Ubuntu 16.04 as an example. Other systems, such as MacOS or Windows, and even other Linux systems, have different installation methods.

We will install everything via Terminal, for which you will require the system's root password.

Install Webserver

Webserver, or HTTP server, is a software that processes requests from browsers. Its primary function is to store, deliver, and process web pages. The most widely used is Apache (https://httpd.apache.org/).

Open your terminal and issue the following command. This will install the latest Apache web server into your system, if it is not already installed.

```
$ sudo apt-get install apache2
```

The result is quite long but should start and finish with something like the following:

```
Reading package lists... Done
Building dependency tree
Reading state information... Done
The following package was automatically installed and is no longer required:

...

Processing triggers for libc-bin (2.23-0ubuntu3) ...
Processing triggers for systemd (229-4ubuntu6) ...
Processing triggers for ureadahead (0.100.0-19) ...
Processing triggers for ufw (0.35-0ubuntu2) ...
```

© Sándor Gömöri 2016
S. Gömöri, *Learn CakePHP*, DOI 10.1007/978-1-4842-1212-7_6

Install MySQL

MySQL is the most popular open source relational database system for web applications. If you require some database in which to store your application's data, MySQL is the easiest option.

Open your terminal and issue the following command to install the MySQL server:

```
$ sudo apt-get install mysql-server
```

This result is also very long, so I cut out the middle.

```
Reading package lists...
Building dependency tree...
Reading state information...
The following package was automatically installed and is no longer required:
  libnghttp2-14

...

Preparing to unpack .../mysql-server_5.7.12-0ubuntu1_all.deb ...
Unpacking mysql-server (5.7.12-0ubuntu1) ...
Setting up mysql-server (5.7.12-0ubuntu1) ...
```

Install PHP

PHP is a server-side scripting language designed mainly for web development. It is very popular: more than 80% of web servers are installed with PHP. It is easy to learn, flexible, and robust, and is perhaps the language behind CakePHP.

The latest version is PHP 7, which represents the next great leap after PHP 5. PHP 7 introduced scalar type declarations, return type declarations, the null coalescing operator, spaceship operator, anonymous classes, and many other features.

PHP should be installed with a few modules, to get everything to work. We will run PHP as an Apache module and install MySQL, mbstring, intl, and xml modules.

```
$ sudo apt-get install php7.0 libapache2-mod-php7.0 php7.0-mysql php7.0-
mbstring php7.0-intl php7.0-xml
```

The output result is also shortened.

```
Reading package lists...
Building dependency tree...
Reading state information...
The following packages were automatically installed and are no longer
required:
  libjs-excanvas mercurial mercurial-common php-cli-prompt php-composer-semver

...
```

Creating config file /etc/php/7.0/mods-available/xsl.ini with new version
Processing triggers for libapache2-mod-php7.0 (7.0.4-7ubuntu2.1) ...

Post Installation

We should enable mod_rewrite to get the best of CakePHP routing. As on a development server, we will install CakePHP into a user directory, so we have to enable and set this up also.

Let's enable userdir first.

```
$ sudo a2enmod userdir
```

Edit /etc/apache2/mods-enabled/userdir.conf and paste the following code:

```
1   <IfModule mod_userdir.c>
2     UserDir public_html
3     UserDir disabled root
4
5     <Directory /home/*/public_html>
6       AllowOverride FileInfo AuthConfig Limit Indexes
7       Options MultiViews Indexes SymLinksIfOwnerMatch IncludesNoExec
8       <Limit GET POST OPTIONS>
9         Require all granted
10      </Limit>
11      <LimitExcept GET POST OPTIONS>
12        Require all denied
13      </LimitExcept>
14    </Directory>
15  </IfModule>
```

The net file to edit is /etc/apache2/mods-available/php7.0.conf. On Ubuntu, running PHP scripts in the user directory is disabled, so we should enable it. Comment out the last five lines of the file.

```
21  #<IfModule mod_userdir.c>
22  #   <Directory /home/*/public_html>
23  #       php_admin_flag engine Off
24  #   </Directory>
25  #</IfModule>
```

Let's enable and set up mod_rewrite.

```
$ sudo a2enmod rewrite
```

To let everything load and work, we should restart Apache.

```
$ sudo service apache2 restart
```

Install Composer

Composer is *the* application-level package manager for PHP and provides a standard format for managing dependencies of PHP software and required libraries. It is an essential tool for any PHP development. As Composer is the recommended way of installing CakePHP, we will install it first.

Open your terminal and issue the following command to download Composer via curl, and install it to the current directory.

```
$ curl -s https://getcomposer.org/installer | php
```

Install CakePHP

As an example, we'll use a blog to familiarize ourselves with CakePHP unit testing. First, create a new CakePHP project with Composer.

```
$ cd ~/public_html
$ php composer.phar create-project --prefer-dist cakephp/app cakeBlog
```

This will create a cakeBlog folder in the current working directory and download the latest version of cakephp (which is 3.2.8 at the time of writing) and all required packages.

After install, you should set write permissions to /tmp and /logs folder for the web server user.

Composer creates a composer.json and a composer.lock file in the project's directory. These files describe the project's identification data, dependencies, and other dependency related settings.

As we enabled the user directory with Apache and PHP, I did this at my home (/home/rrd) directory's public_html folder, so I will access my app at http://localhost/~rrd/cakeBlog/ and use this URL in my examples.

If everything is OK, you should be able to navigate to your install path through your browser. You'll see something such as in Figure 6-1.

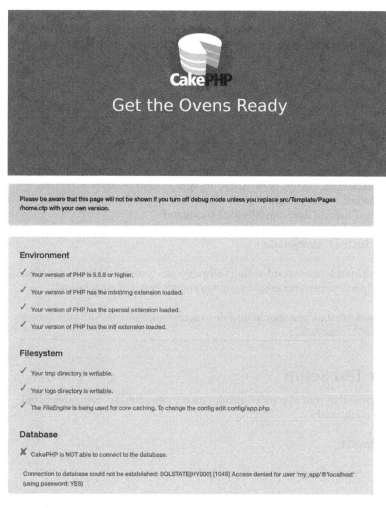

Figure 6-1. *My blog after install*

Do not worry about the error message regarding the database connection. I will get back to that soon.

Installing PHPUnit

PHPUnit is the de facto standard for unit testing in PHP. PHPUnit is integrated into CakePHP for unit testing. Thanks to Composer, it is really simple to install with all of its required packages. We do not need PHPUnit on the production server, so we will use the --dev option.

```
$ cd ~/public_html/cakeBlog
$ php composer.phar require --dev phpunit/phpunit
```

33

If you use the --dev option, Composer will put this dependency into composer. json's require-dev section. Then, on the production server, you can skip installation of these dependencies, which are required only for development, by using the following command:

```
$ php composer.phar --no-dev install
```

Install phpMyAdmin

phpMyAdmin is a free and open source tool written in PHP for the administration of MySQL with the use of a web browser. It can perform various tasks, such as creating, modifying, or deleting databases, tables, fields, or rows; executing SQL statements; or managing users and permissions.

Open your terminal and issue the following command:

```
$ sudo apt-get install phpmyadmin
```

It will start the installation wizard, which will guide you throughout the installation process. Choose Apache when you are prompted to choose between Apache and Lighttpd.

After a successful install, you should be able to access phpMyAdmin with your browser at http://localhost/phpmyadmin.

Check Your Test Setup

To check if all went well in your app root directory (in my case, public_html/cakeBlog), run the following command:

```
$ vendor/bin/phpunit
```

You should see something similar to Figure 6-2.

```
rrd@rrd-ubuntu: ~/public_html/cakeBlog
rrd@rrd-ubuntu:~/public_html/cakeBlog$ vendor/bin/phpunit
PHPUnit 5.3.2 by Sebastian Bergmann and contributors.

...                                                          3 / 3 (100%)

Time: 266 ms, Memory: 10.00Mb

OK (3 tests, 18 assertions)
rrd@rrd-ubuntu:~/public_html/cakeBlog$
```

Figure 6-2. *PHPUnit first test*

You may receive error messages such as the following:

Warning Error: SplFileInfo::openFile(/home/rrd/public_html/cakeBlog/tmp/
cache/persistent/myapp_cake_core_translations_cake_en__u_s): failed to open
stream: Permission denied in [/home/rrd/public_html/cakeBlog/vendor/cakephp/
cakephp/src/Cache/Engine/FileEngine.php, line 395]

This means that you do not have write access to different files in your cake tmp directory, located at cakeBlog/tmp. For example, on Ubuntu, these files are owned by the www-data user and its group. You should add yourself to this group, or set yourself as the owner of tmp recursively. If at any time you get permission errors, check the tmp folder first, as many new files will have been created here.

Figure 6-2 shows that the three tests ran successfully with eighteen assertions. These three tests are automatically generated for PagesController. The corresponding test file is located at /tests/TestCase/Controller/PagesControllerTest.php. You can take a look if you want. Soon, I will describe what is in that file. For now, it is enough to know that green is good. We got a green bar at the end of the tests, so we are good.

Preparing

We should set up a few things, so that we can begin unit testing.

Set Debug Level

In /config/app.php, your debug level is set to true by default.

'debug' => filter_var(env('DEBUG', true), FILTER_VALIDATE_BOOLEAN),

Leave it like this for now. It is not mandatory for unit testing, but error and debug messages can help as much in testing as in coding.

Set Up Test Database

If your application interacts with a database (and most of the apps will), you'll need a default and a test database. All your database-related tests will use the test database.

CakePHP will remove tables from your database at the end of test runs. So **DO**

NOT use the same database for default and test; otherwise, you will lose data without any warning.

Find the Datasources definition in your /config/app.php file and change at least the username, password, and database values for your default and test data sources. Let's say my default database is cake_blog, its username is rrd, and the password is Gouranga. My test database is cake_blog_test, with the same username and password.

app.php

```
1   'Datasources' => [
2       'default' => [
3           'className' => 'Cake\Database\Connection',
4           'driver' => 'Cake\Database\Driver\Mysql',
5           'persistent' => false,
6           'host' => 'localhost',
7           //'port' => 'non_standard_port_number',
8           'username' => 'rrd',
9           'password' => 'Gouranga',
10          'database' => 'cake_blog',
11          'encoding' => 'utf8',
12          'timezone' => 'UTC',
13          'flags' => [],
14          'cacheMetadata' => true,
15          'log' => false,
16          'quoteIdentifiers' => false,
17
18          //'init' => ['SET GLOBAL innodb_stats_on_metadata = 0'],
19
20          'url' => env('DATABASE_URL', null),
21      ],
22
23      /**
24       * The test connection is used during the test suite.
25       */
26      'test' => [
27          'className' => 'Cake\Database\Connection',
28          'driver' => 'Cake\Database\Driver\Mysql',
29          'persistent' => false,
30          'host' => 'localhost',
31          //'port' => 'non_standard_port_number',
32          'username' => 'rrd',
33          'password' => 'Gouranga',
```

```
34              'database' => 'cake_blog_test',
35              'encoding' => 'utf8',
36              'timezone' => 'UTC',
37              'cacheMetadata' => true,
38              'quoteIdentifiers' => false,
39              'log' => false,
40              //'init' => ['SET GLOBAL innodb_stats_on_metadata = 0'],
41              'url' => env('DATABASE_TEST_URL', null),
42          ],
43      ],
```

For our blog, we want to handle users, who can write posts and comment on their own and other's posts. Posts can be tagged and categorized. After some planning, we end up with the database schema shown on Figure 6-3.

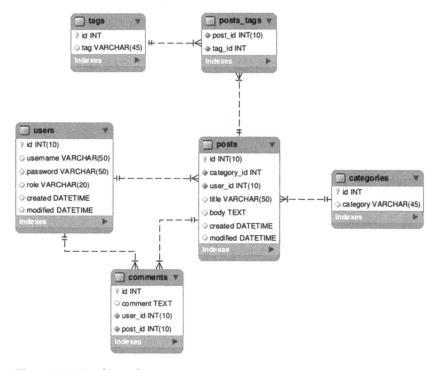

Figure 6-3. *Database schema*

The default data source will be used by your application and the test data source by the tests. The keys are self-descriptive. They define which class and driver is used to access the database, the connection type, host and port, the database name, the MySQL user and password, the character encoding, and so on.

Open your browser, navigate to localhost/phpmyadmin (http://phpmyadmin.net), and create both default and test databases. You can do this by selecting database from the top tabs and then using the create database form. Alternatively, select SQL from the top tabs and copy and paste.

Use the following SQL statement to create the two databases and their tables:

```
1   SET @OLD_UNIQUE_CHECKS=@@UNIQUE_CHECKS, UNIQUE_CHECKS=0;
2   SET @OLD_FOREIGN_KEY_CHECKS=@@FOREIGN_KEY_CHECKS,
3     FOREIGN_KEY_CHECKS=0;
4   SET @OLD_SQL_MODE=@@SQL_MODE, SQL_MODE='TRADITIONAL';
5
6   CREATE SCHEMA IF NOT EXISTS `cake_blog`
7     DEFAULT CHARACTER SET latin1;
```

First, we create the default database, which is cake_blog.

```
8   USE `cake_blog`;
9
10  -- ---------------------------------------------------------
11  -- Table `cake_blog`.`users`
12  -- ---------------------------------------------------------
13  CREATE TABLE IF NOT EXISTS `cake_blog`.`users` (
14    `id` INT(10) UNSIGNED NOT NULL AUTO_INCREMENT ,
15    `username` VARCHAR(50) NULL DEFAULT NULL ,
16    `password` VARCHAR(50) NULL DEFAULT NULL ,
17    `role` VARCHAR(20) NULL DEFAULT NULL ,
18    `created` DATETIME NULL DEFAULT NULL ,
19    `modified` DATETIME NULL DEFAULT NULL ,
20    PRIMARY KEY (`id`) )
21  ENGINE = InnoDB
22  DEFAULT CHARACTER SET = latin1;
23
```

Then we add the users' table, which is used for storing our blog's users.

```
24
25  -- ---------------------------------------------------------
26  -- Table `cake_blog`.`categories`
27  -- ---------------------------------------------------------
28  CREATE TABLE IF NOT EXISTS `cake_blog`.`categories` (
29    `id` INT UNSIGNED NOT NULL AUTO_INCREMENT ,
30    `category` VARCHAR(45) NULL ,
31    PRIMARY KEY (`id`) )
32  ENGINE = InnoDB;
33
```

Our blog post could be associated with categories, so we create a database table for categories.

```
34
35   -- ---------------------------------------------------------
36   -- Table `cake_blog`.`posts`
37   -- ---------------------------------------------------------
38   CREATE TABLE IF NOT EXISTS `cake_blog`.`posts` (
39     `id` INT(10) UNSIGNED NOT NULL AUTO_INCREMENT ,
40     `category_id` INT UNSIGNED NOT NULL ,
41     `user_id` INT(10) UNSIGNED NOT NULL ,
42     `title` VARCHAR(50) NULL DEFAULT NULL ,
43     `body` TEXT NULL DEFAULT NULL ,
44     `created` DATETIME NULL DEFAULT NULL ,
45     `modified` DATETIME NULL DEFAULT NULL ,
46     PRIMARY KEY (`id`) ,
47     INDEX `fk_posts_users` (`user_id` ASC) ,
48     INDEX `fk_posts_categories1` (`category_id` ASC) ,
49     CONSTRAINT `fk_posts_users`
50       FOREIGN KEY (`user_id` )
51       REFERENCES `cake_blog`.`users` (`id` )
52       ON DELETE RESTRICT
53       ON UPDATE RESTRICT,
54     CONSTRAINT `fk_posts_categories1`
55       FOREIGN KEY (`category_id` )
56       REFERENCES `cake_blog`.`categories` (`id` )
57       ON DELETE RESTRICT
58       ON UPDATE RESTRICT)
59   ENGINE = InnoDB
60   AUTO_INCREMENT = 4
61   DEFAULT CHARACTER SET = latin1;
62
```

The blog posts also should be stored in a database table. We added indexes for user_id and category_id fields and foreign keys to these.

```
63
64   -- ---------------------------------------------------------
65   -- Table `cake_blog`.`tags`
66   -- ---------------------------------------------------------
67   CREATE TABLE IF NOT EXISTS `cake_blog`.`tags` (
68     `id` INT UNSIGNED NOT NULL AUTO_INCREMENT ,
69     `tag` VARCHAR(45) NULL ,
70     PRIMARY KEY (`id`) )
71   ENGINE = InnoDB;
72
```

We want to use tagging on our posts, so we need a table for the tags also.

```
73
74  -- ----------------------------------------------------
75  -- Table `cake_blog`.`posts_tags`
76  -- ----------------------------------------------------
77  CREATE TABLE IF NOT EXISTS `cake_blog`.`posts_tags` (
78    `id` INT UNSIGNED NOT NULL AUTO_INCREMENT,
79    `post_id` INT(10) UNSIGNED NOT NULL ,
80    `tag_id` INT UNSIGNED NOT NULL ,
81    PRIMARY KEY (`id`),
82    INDEX `fk_posts_has_tags_tags1` (`tag_id` ASC) ,
83    INDEX `fk_posts_has_tags_posts1` (`post_id` ASC) ,
84    CONSTRAINT `fk_posts_has_tags_posts1`
85      FOREIGN KEY (`post_id` )
86      REFERENCES `cake_blog`.`posts` (`id` )
87      ON DELETE RESTRICT
88      ON UPDATE RESTRICT,
89    CONSTRAINT `fk_posts_has_tags_tags1`
90      FOREIGN KEY (`tag_id` )
91      REFERENCES `cake_blog`.`tags` (`id` )
92      ON DELETE RESTRICT
93      ON UPDATE RESTRICT)
94  ENGINE = InnoDB
95  DEFAULT CHARACTER SET = latin1;
96
```

The next thing is to create the join table between the posts and tags tables.

```
97
98   -- ----------------------------------------------------
99   -- Table `cake_blog`.`comments`
100  -- ----------------------------------------------------
101  CREATE TABLE IF NOT EXISTS `cake_blog`.`comments` (
102    `id` INT UNSIGNED NOT NULL AUTO_INCREMENT ,
103    `comment` TEXT NULL ,
104    `user_id` INT(10) UNSIGNED NOT NULL ,
105    `post_id` INT(10) UNSIGNED NOT NULL ,
106    PRIMARY KEY (`id`) ,
107    INDEX `fk_comments_users1` (`user_id` ASC) ,
108    INDEX `fk_comments_posts1` (`post_id` ASC) ,
109    CONSTRAINT `fk_comments_users1`
110      FOREIGN KEY (`user_id` )
111      REFERENCES `cake_blog`.`users` (`id` )
112      ON DELETE RESTRICT
113      ON UPDATE RESTRICT,
114    CONSTRAINT `fk_comments_posts1`
115      FOREIGN KEY (`post_id` )
```

```
116       REFERENCES `cake_blog`.`posts` (`id` )
117       ON DELETE RESTRICT
118       ON UPDATE RESTRICT)
119   ENGINE = InnoDB;
120
121
```

Finally, we create the comments table, on which comments will be stored.

```
122
123   SET SQL_MODE=@OLD_SQL_MODE;
124   SET FOREIGN_KEY_CHECKS=@OLD_FOREIGN_KEY_CHECKS;
125   SET UNIQUE_CHECKS=@OLD_UNIQUE_CHECKS;
126
```

As the last step, we have to create the test database also. For now, cake_blog_test is OK without any database table.

```
127   CREATE SCHEMA IF NOT EXISTS `cake_blog_test`
128       DEFAULT CHARACTER SET latin1;
```
cake_blog.sql

If all went as planned, you should see something such as appears in Figure 6-4.

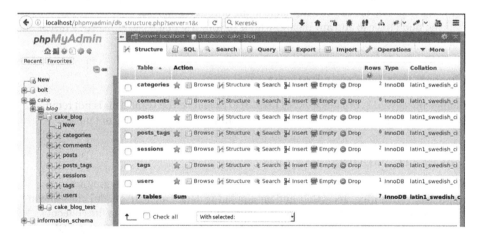

Figure 6-4. *phpMyAdmin after database creation*

Set Up Session Handling

Just as we would in real-world middle-size applications, we'll use CakePHP's database session handling for this project.

CakePHP give us four different ready-to-use session-handling mechanisms.

The default is php, where session handling is done by PHP in a way php.ini defines. I normally do not choose this option.

The second option is cake, whereby session data will be stored in files in the /tmp/sessions folder. I use this option when the application is really simple and does not use any database.

The third option is database, when session data is stored in a database at a table named sessions. I use this in most cases.

The last option is cache, whereby sessions are stored in a cache such as APC, Memcached, or XCache. This option is recommended if you are planning to have an application with high usage.

Cake makes it super easy to change session handling at any time. So, as your application popularity grows, you can switch from database to cache.

Open your /config/app.php file and change the default value to database for session handling.

```
1  'Session' => [
2       'defaults' => 'database',
3  ],
```

The SQL script for database tables for sessions is located at app/config/schema/sessions.sql. You should add this table to the default database.

You don't have to add any database table to your test database. CakePHP's Test Suite will do this automatically.

Create the Default Layout

Change the default.ctp file at /src/Template/Layout, if you want. This is not required, but at some point, we'll want to change CakePHP's default layout. Why not now?

CakePHP Models

Models are the *M* in MVC. They are the basis of our web application, as they are responsible for storing, accessing, and manipulating data. CakePHP's Model class files are split between Table and Entity objects. Table objects provide access to the collection of entities stored in a specific table. CakePHP supports MySQL, SQLite, PostgreSQL, SQLServer, and Oracle.

Models extend CakePHP's Model class, so they are equipped with a lot of features out of the box. They have events such as Model.beforeFind, Model.beforeSave, Model.afterSave, and others. They have inherited methods such as find(), get(), save(), and so on.

Database Queries

The most widely used model method is find(), which returns a query object.

```
1  $query = $posts
2      ->find()
3      ->select(['id', 'title'])
4      ->where(['id <' => 100])
5      ->order(['created' => 'DESC']);
```

As you can see, find() can be chained with other model methods, such as select(), where(), etc. This is a new feature of CakePHP 3's new object-relational mapping (ORM) feature, which is really handy and self-descriptive. With this query, we can select id and title of posts, whose ids are smaller than 100, and the result set will be ordered by the created field. This query will generate something similar to the following SQL statement:

```
SELECT id, title FROM posts WHERE id < 100 ORDER BY created DESC;
```

Query objects can be modified later, as they actually execute if we call execute() or iterate over the query or call all().

Model Associations

Relations between database tables are handled by model associations in CakePHP applications. There are four association types. One-to-one relationships are handled by the hasOne association, one-to-many relationships by hasMany, many-to-one relationships by belongsTo, and many-to-many relationships by belongsToMany.

HasOne Associations

In our blog database, there is no hasOne association. We can create a profiles database table and model, and if a user has only one profile, he or she is in a hasOne association with the profile. In this case, the profile table should have a user_id field for describing the link between it and the user.

HasMany Associations

In our blog database categories, hasMany posts means that a category can have many posts.

BelongsTo Associations

This is the other end of a hasOne or hasMany association. So, in the previous examples, a profile belongsTo a user and a post belongsTo a category.

BelongsToMany associations

In our blog database, there is a belongsToMany association between posts and tags, meaning that a post can have many tags and a tag can be assigned to many posts.

CakePHP Controllers

Controllers are the *C* in MVC. Controllers are the middleware between models and views. Your controller should handle interpreting the request data. Commonly, a controller is used to manage the logic for one model.

Controllers should extend Cake's Controller class. Controllers provide a number of methods. These are called *actions*. By default, each public method in a controller is an action and is accessible from a URL. An action is responsible for interpreting the request and creating the response and setting up variables for the view.

CakePHP Views

Views are the *V* in MVC. Views are for presenting the response, mainly meaning to create an HTML document. A layout is the main container for views. Each controller action should have its corresponding view file at /src/Template/ folder.

Let's see how to create models, controllers, and views automatically.

Baking

In my opinion, one of the best features of CakePHP is baking, which is itself worth writing a book about.

I will not go into detail here, but bake is a tool for automatically generating basic code four your blog. With bake, you can automatically generate model, controller, and template files and many others, such as fixtures, shells, etc.

Open a terminal, go into your app folder, and start CakePHP's bake script.

```
1  $ cd ~/public_html/cakeBlog/
2  $ bin/cake bake
```

If you see an error message about file permissions, just ignore it. Because the web server usually runs as a different user than yourself, it has different file permissions. You can get rid of these error messages by manually emptying your app/tmp/cache folder's subfolders or fixing its permissions.

You'll see the screen shown in Figure 6-5.

```
rrd@rrd-ubuntu:~$ cd public_html/cakeBlog/
rrd@rrd-ubuntu:~/public_html/cakeBlog$ bin/cake bake

Welcome to CakePHP v3.2.7 Console
------------------------------------------------------------
App : src
Path: /home/rrd/public_html/cakeBlog/src/
PHP : 7.0.5-3+donate.sury.org~wily+1
------------------------------------------------------------
The following commands can be used to generate skeleton code for your application.

Available bake commands:

- all
- behavior
- cell
- component
- controller
- fixture
- form
- helper
- mailer
- migration
- migration_snapshot
- model
- plugin
- seed
- shell
- shell_helper
- task
- template
- test

By using `cake bake [name]` you can invoke a specific bake task.
```

Figure 6-5. *bake script in action*

Now let's generate all model table and entity files, corresponding fixtures, and test files at once. For this, we will use the model all parameters for bake. This will create files at /src/Model/Entity, /src/Model/Table, /tests/Fixture, and /tests/TestCase/ Model/Table. Bake will generate one file for each database table in each of these folders.

```
1  $ bin/cake bake model all
```

We can use the same process for our controllers and views. With the following commands, all controller and view files will be created by bake:

```
1  $ bin/cake controller all
2  $ bin/cake template all
```

If you receive an error message such as Error: Cannot generate views for models with no primary key, it is because of the session model. In this case, bake your tags and users template manually.

```
1  $ bin/cake template tags
2  $ bin/cake template users
```

Clean It Up

Some files are unnecessary and should be deleted. Bake generates files for sessions and join tables. As our blog will be very simple, we do not want anything extra with join tables, so we do not need these files.

- `src/Controller/PostsTagsController.php`

- `src/Controller/SessionsController.php`

- `src/Model/Entity/Session.php`

- `src/Model/Table/SessionsTable.php`

- `tests/TestCase/Controller/SessionsControllerTest.php`

- `tests/TestCase/Controller/PostsTagsControllerTest.php`

- `tests/TestCase/Model/Table/SessionsTableTest.php`

- `tests/Fixture/SessionsFixture.php`

You can bake your models *before* you add the session table to your database. In this case, session-related files will not be generated, so you don't have to delete them.

You can bake your models, controllers, and views without the `all` parameter and then choose your objects one by one. You can also skip the `join` model, so that nothing will be generated for `PostsTags`.

I think my approach is the fastest of these three options.

Let's Play

Browse to `http://localhost/~rrd/cakeBlog/users`. You should see something similar than Figure 6-6, and be able to add a user.

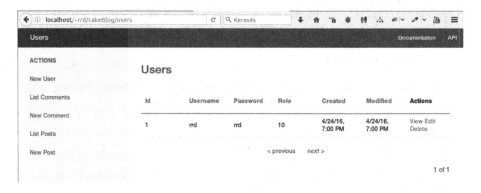

Figure 6-6. *Baked Users page*

You can add, modify, and delete categories, tags, posts, and comments also. And all of this code is generated automatically by bake. We did not write a single line of code yet. Cool, huh?

Run vendor/bin/phpunit again, to check if all went well. In Figure 6-7, dots are the successful test; *I*'s are the incomplete ones.

Do not worry about incomplete tests for now. So, bake generated 43 tests. Of these, 18 are assertions and 40 are incomplete tests.

```
rrd@rrd-ubuntu:~/public_html/cakeBlog$ vendor/bin/phpunit
PHPUnit 5.3.2 by Sebastian Bergmann and contributors.

IIIIIIIIII...IIIIIIIIIIIIIIIIIIIIIIIIIIIII                43 / 43 (100%)

Time: 3.35 minutes, Memory: 12.00Mb

OK, but incomplete, skipped, or risky tests!
Tests: 43, Assertions: 18, Incomplete: 40.
```

Figure 6-7. *Tests after code generation with* bake

It is now time to see what is what here. Let's start with test data fixtures.

Summary

In this chapter, we took a closer look at testing. We installed all the necessary servers, PHP, and Composer and created our application skeleton, via Composer, and our databases. You learned how to use the bake script to automatically generate code. We also set up a session-handling method for our blog.

Felix always felt he was a little bit different

CHAPTER 7

Fixtures

Most of the time, an application will manipulate data. Users will add new posts and comments or edit them, admins will create new tags and categories, etc. Fixtures are sample data generated for test cases. Why do we need them? Playing with application data is a bad idea. We could accidentally delete or modify data during development. We could also break database relations. Not a good idea. Fixtures are another layer of isolation. A *smaller* and *cleaner* data set helps to make sure our code returns expected results and runs fast. Definitely a good idea.

CakePHP uses the connection named $test in your config/app.php configuration file. CakePHP creates tables for the fixtures, populates the tables with data, and (after running test methods) empties the fixture tables and removes fixture tables from the test database.

Creating Fixtures

There are several ways to create fixtures. You should create your fixtures in the /app/Test/Fixture folder.

On the Fly

Because we baked our models, we already have fixture files at /tests/Fixture, such as UsersFixture.php. Let's check what we generated earlier.

```
1   <?php
2   namespace App\Test\Fixture;
3
4   use Cake\TestSuite\Fixture\TestFixture;
5
6   /**
7    * UsersFixture
8    *
9    */
10  class UsersFixture extends TestFixture
```

© Sándor Gömöri 2016
S. Gömöri, *Learn CakePHP*, DOI 10.1007/978-1-4842-1212-7_7

```
11  {
12
13      /**
14       * Fields
15       *
16       * @var array
17       */
18      // @codingStandardsIgnoreStart
19      public $fields = [
20          'id' => [
21              'type' => 'integer', 'length' => 10, 'unsigned' => true,
22              'null' => false, 'default' => null, 'comment' => '',
23              'autoIncrement' => true, 'precision' => null
24              ],
25          'username' => [
26              'type' => 'string', 'length' => 50, 'null' => true,
27              'default' => null, 'comment' => '', 'precision' => null,
28              'fixed' => null
29              ],
30          'password' => [
31              'type' => 'string', 'length' => 50, 'null' => true,
32              'default' => null, 'comment' => '', 'precision' => null,
33              'fixed' => null
34              ],
35          'role' => [
36              'type' => 'string', 'length' => 20, 'null' => true,
37              'default' => null, 'comment' => '', 'precision' => null,
38              'fixed' => null
39              ],
40          'created' => [
41              'type' => 'datetime', 'length' => null, 'null' => true,
42              'default' => null, 'comment' => '', 'precision' => null
43              ],
44          'modified' => [
45              'type' => 'datetime', 'length' => null, 'null' => true,
46              'default' => null, 'comment' => '', 'precision' => null
47              ],
48          '_constraints' => [
49              'primary' => [
50                  'type' => 'primary', 'columns' => ['id'], 'length' => []
51                  ],
52          ],
53          '_options' => [
54              'engine' => 'InnoDB',
55              'collation' => 'latin1_swedish_ci'
56          ],
57      ];
```

```
58        // @codingStandardsIgnoreEnd
59
60        /**
61         * Records
62         *
63         * @var array
64         */
65        public $records = [
66            [
67                'id' => 1,
68                'username' => 'Lorem ipsum dolor sit amet',
69                'password' => 'Lorem ipsum dolor sit amet',
70                'role' => 'Lorem ipsum dolor ',
71                'created' => '2016-04-24 18:39:32',
72                'modified' => '2016-04-24 18:39:32'
73            ],
74        ];
75    }
```

The $fields array describes the table schema for the model Users. It describes all the fields, their data types and length, default value, and some other values. It also adds used indexes.

The $records array contains one sample record, but you can add as many as you want. Using this approach, you can start writing unit tests *before* you have anything in your application's database—even before you have a database at all. It's really useful in the early stages of development to test database structure changes.

At later development phases, when the database structure is finalized, it is also essential for testing to have records that will not change.

When you run a test in which this fixture is imported, Cake will create a Users table in the test database, with the fields described here, and insert records from the $records array. The model tests will use this data during testing.

You can also use dynamic data in your fixtures. For this, just use the init() function.

```
1    <?php
2    namespace App\Test\Fixture;
3
4    use Cake\TestSuite\Fixture\TestFixture;
5
6    /**
7     * UsersFixture
8     *
9     */
10   class UsersFixture extends TestFixture
11   {
12
13       /**
14        * Fields
15        *
```

```
16          * @var array
17          */
18         // @codingStandardsIgnoreStart
19         public $fields = [
20             'id' => [
21                 'type' => 'integer', 'length' => 10, 'unsigned' => true,
22                 'null' => false, 'default' => null, 'comment' => '',
23                 'autoIncrement' => true, 'precision' => null
24                 ],
25             'username' => [
26                 'type' => 'string', 'length' => 50, 'null' => true,
27                 'default' => null, 'comment' => '', 'precision' => null,
28                 'fixed' => null
29                 ],
30             'password' => [
31                 'type' => 'string', 'length' => 50, 'null' => true,
32                 'default' => null, 'comment' => '', 'precision' => null,
33                 'fixed' => null
34                 ],
35             'role' => [
36                 'type' => 'string', 'length' => 20, 'null' => true,
37                 'default' => null, 'comment' => '', 'precision' => null,
38                 'fixed' => null
39                 ],
40             'created' => [
41                 'type' => 'datetime', 'length' => null, 'null' => true,
42                 'default' => null, 'comment' => '', 'precision' => null
43                 ],
44             'modified' => [
45                 'type' => 'datetime', 'length' => null, 'null' => true,
46                 'default' => null, 'comment' => '', 'precision' => null
47                 ],
48             '_constraints' => [
49                 'primary' => [
50                     'type' => 'primary', 'columns' => ['id'], 'length' => []
51                     ],
52             ],
53             '_options' => [
54                 'engine' => 'InnoDB',
55                 'collation' => 'latin1_swedish_ci'
56             ],
57         ];
58         // @codingStandardsIgnoreEnd
59
60         public function init()
61         {
62                 $this->records = [
63                     [
```

```
64                        'id' => 1,
65                        'username' => 'Lorem ipsum dolor sit amet',
66                        'password' => 'Lorem ipsum dolor sit amet',
67                        'role' => 'Lorem ipsum dolor ',
68                        'created' => date('Y-m-d H:i:s'),
69                        'modified' => date('Y-m-d H:i:s')
70                    ],
71            ];
72        }
73  }
```

As you can see, the beginning of the file is the same as in the previous example. But after we create the $fields array, we do not create a $records array, but create it at the init() method. We do this because we want to insert dynamic data into created and modified fields. So, these data will be different on every test run, based on current system time.

Importing the Existing Model Schema

If you've already created database models, you can import them to your fixture without any existing data records. This can be useful in early development stages, when the database structure tends to change frequently. Without this, all database changes should be manually changed in fixtures also. It adds some overhead, so at later development phases, the previous examples will be faster.

```
1  <?php
2  class UsersFixture extends TestFixture {
3        public $import = ['model' => 'Users'];
4  }
5  ?>
```

If you have tables but no models, you should use the following code sample. It is useful when you create plugins or libraries.

```
1  <?php
2  class UsersFixture extends TestFixture {
3        public $import = ['table' => 'users'];
4  }
5  ?>
```

Don't forget to manually add records to your fixtures. As tests should run as fast as possible, try to have just enough records. Do not forget: Inserting and removing test records takes time. More records require more time, so add just enough records as is absolutely necessary. Let's say somewhere in our application we would like to list all users whose names start with a given letter. We would have a getUsersByName($ch) method in our model that will handle this.

In this scenario, we should have at least three records in our user fixture with different usernames.

```
65      public $records = [
66          [
67              'id' => 1,
68              'username' => 'rrd',
69              'password' => 'Lorem ipsum dolor sit amet',
70              'role' => 'Lorem ipsum dolor ',
71              'created' => '2016-04-24 18:39:32',
72              'modified' => '2016-04-24 18:39:32'
73          ],
74          [
75              'id' => 2,
76              'username' => 'gauranga',
77              'password' => 'Lorem ipsum dolor sit amet',
78              'role' => 'Lorem ipsum dolor ',
79              'created' => '2016-04-24 18:39:32',
80              'modified' => '2016-04-24 18:39:32'
81          ],
74          [
75              'id' => 3,
76              'username' => 'r2d2',
77              'password' => 'Lorem ipsum dolor sit amet',
78              'role' => 'Lorem ipsum dolor ',
79              'created' => '2016-04-24 18:39:32',
80              'modified' => '2016-04-24 18:39:32'
81          ],
82      ];
```

As we have these three records, we can write tests for getUsersByName($ch). If $ch is "g," we should get record 2; if $ch is "r," we should get records 1 and 3 and should not get any records otherwise.

If you do not like entering records manually, you can import them from an existing database table, with phpMyAdmin. Just use the export function and choose PHP array as the format of the export, as shown in Figure 7-1.

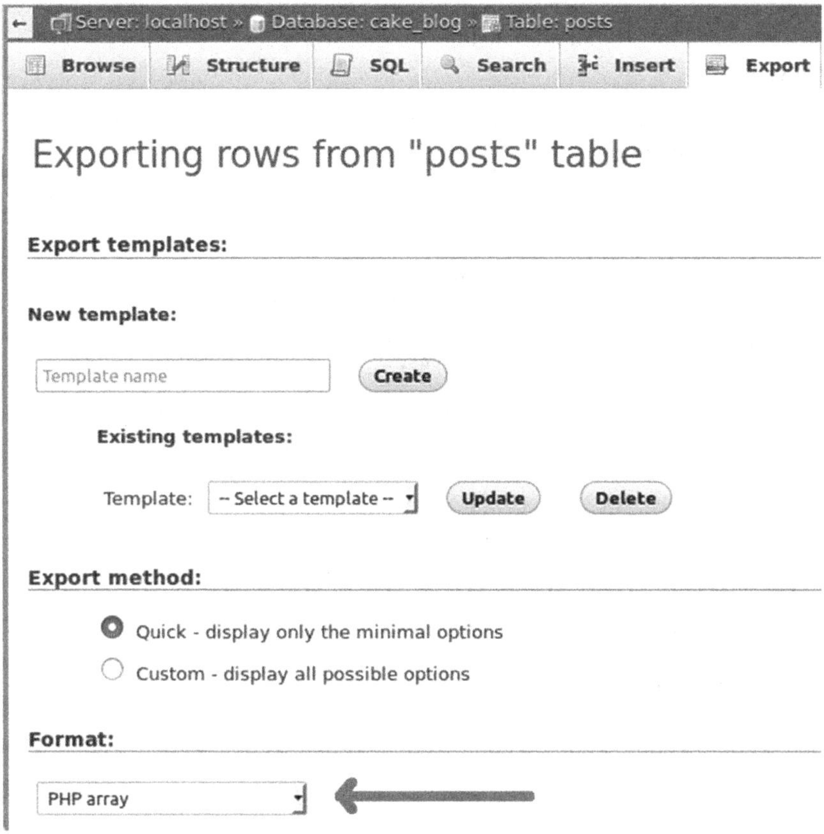

Figure 7-1. *Export records by phpMyAdmin*

This will create an array for you that can be copy-pasted as your $records array. This makes it easy to have a lot of records, but still try to have as few as you can.

Loading Fixtures into Your Tests

Let's take a look at tests/TestCase/Model/Table/UsersTableTest.php, which is also generated by bake, as discussed in the previous chapter.

```
1   <?php
2   namespace App\Test\TestCase\Model\Table;
3
```

Namespaces are added at PHP 5.3, as well as a recommended language feature to use in PHP 7 applications. The simplest definition of a namespace is that it is a way of encapsulating items.

```
4   use App\Model\Table\UsersTable;
5   use Cake\ORM\TableRegistry;
6   use Cake\TestSuite\TestCase;
7
```

By the use operator, we import other namespaces.

```
8   /**
9    * App\Model\Table\UsersTable Test Case
10   */
11  class UsersTableTest extends TestCase
12  {
13
```

Model tests extend CakePHP's TestCase class.

```
14      /**
15       * Test subject
16       *
17       * @var \App\Model\Table\UsersTable
18       */
19      public $Users;
20
21      /**
22       * Fixtures
23       *
24       * @var array
25       */
26      public $fixtures = [
27          'app.users',
28          'app.comments',
29          'app.posts',
30          'app.categories',
31          'app.tags',
32          'app.posts_tags'
33      ];
34
```

The $fixtures array defines which fixtures should be loaded for our tests. As you can see, bake imported fixtures related to the User model. For now, get rid of the related models and keep it simple. Change the code to look like this:

```
26  public $fixtures = ['app.users'];
```

If you do not have any model queries that will try to retrieve related database tables, this will suffice. As only those fixtures will be loaded into your test database that are added here, related database tables will not exist, so trying to query them will create an error.

It is always good practice to keep tests simple and load only fixtures that are absolutely necessary.

Summary

In this chapter, you were introduced to the concept of fixtures and learned how to write, generate, and load them into our tests. One of the most important lessons is to keep fixtures as short as possible and load only the necessary fixtures into your tests.

We're big fans of fat models

CHAPTER 8

Model Tests

OK. I won't torture you anymore. Let's write our first unit test.
Use the following sample code in your `UserFixture.php` file.

```php
1   <?php
2   namespace App\Test\Fixture;
3
4   use Cake\TestSuite\Fixture\TestFixture;
5
6   class UsersFixture extends TestFixture
7   {
8
9       public $import = ['model' => 'Users'];
10
11      public $records = [
12          [
13              'id' => 1,
14              'username' => 'rrd',
15              'password' => 'Gouranga',
16              'role' => 'admin',
17              'created' => '2016-05-01 12:00:00',
18              'modified' => '2016-05-01 12:00:00'
19          ],
20      ];
21  }
```

As you can see, it is really simple. We import the `Users` model and create only one record, meaning one user.

Let's say we want to show who the last registered user is. As we are working with test-driven development (TDD), first we create the test. Open `/tests/TestCase/Model/Table/UsersTableTest.php` and add our first test function to the end of the file.

```
1   public function testIfWeGetRrdAsLastRegisteredUser()
2   {
3       $actual = $this->Users->getLastRegistered();
4       $expected = 'rrd';
5       $this->assertEquals($expected, $actual->username);
6   }
```

I should probably explain this a little. But before we get into it, create the model method itself and run the test.

Because we're big fans of fat models, we'll put this functionality into our Users model. Open /src/Model/Table/UsersTable.php and add a new function to the end of the file.

```
1   public function getLastRegistered(){
2       return true;
3   }
```

It's dumb but exactly what we need at this point. Let's run it. The result should be similar to that shown in Figure 8-1.

```
$ cd ~/public_html/cakeBlog
$ vendor/bin/phpunit --filter testIfWeGetRrdAsLastRegisteredUser tests/
TestCase/Model/Table/UsersTableTest.php
```

```
rrd@rrd-ubuntu:~/public_html/cakeBlog$ vendor/bin/phpunit --filter testIfWeGetRr
dAsLastRegisteredUser tests/TestCase/Model/Table/UsersTableTest.php
PHPUnit 5.3.2 by Sebastian Bergmann and contributors.

Notice Error: Trying to get property of non-object in [/home/rrd/public_html/cak
eBlog/tests/TestCase/Model/Table/UsersTableTest.php, line 90]

F                                                                1 / 1 (100%)

Time: 856 ms, Memory: 8.00Mb

There was 1 failure:

1) App\Test\TestCase\Model\Table\UsersTableTest::testIfWeGetRrdAsLastRegisteredU
ser
Failed asserting that null matches expected 'rrd'.

/home/rrd/public_html/cakeBlog/tests/TestCase/Model/Table/UsersTableTest.php:90

FAILURES!
Tests: 1, Assertions: 1, Failures: 1.
```

Figure 8-1. *Failed test*

Congratulations! You just wrote your first unit test. Let's explore what happened here and why we are happy about a failing test.

 You may receive error messages such as the following:

```
Warning Error: SplFileInfo::openFile(/home/rrd/public_html/cakeBlog/tmp/
cache/models/myapp_cake_model_default_users): failed to open stream:
Permission denied in [/home/rrd/public_html/cakeBlog/vendor/cakephp/cakephp/
src/Cache/Engine/FileEngine.php, line 395]
```

This means you do not have permission to write cache files. Change the permissions and ownerships of all the files in your /tmp folder.

Names of Test Functions

Test function names should start with test.

Don't be afraid to use descriptive function names, even if they are long. They're a great help. We want to check who was the last registered user, and from our fixture, we know that should be our only user 'rrd'. So, we used testIfWeGetRrdAsLastRegisteredUser for the method name. We should keep in mind that when we add new users to our fixtures, we should update this test also.

Assertions

In test functions, we'll do something simple: take an expected value and see if our function's return value is equal to that value. There are other useful assertion methods, such as assertTrue, assertFalse, and assertContains. You can see all of them at PHPUnit API (https://phpunit.de/manual/current/en/appendixes.assertions.html).

Fail First

Do you remember the process of TDD? First, you write a test that fails. We are ready for that, and it should come as a surprise, as our model method only returns true. So, now let's write the correct code.

Passing Test

OK. Our test failed. Now add the actual code to the user model.

```
1  public function getLastRegistered()
2  {
3      return $this->find()
4          ->order('created')
5          ->first();
6  }
```

We requested the last registered user's data by calling the Users model's find() method, ordered the results by created field and returned the first result.

Rerunning the test should give us a passed tests report with a green bar (Figure 8-2).

```
rrd@rrd-ubuntu:~/public_html/cakeBlog$ vendor/bin/phpunit --filter testIfWeGetRr
dAsLastRegisteredUser tests/TestCase/Model/Table/UsersTableTest.php
PHPUnit 5.3.2 by Sebastian Bergmann and contributors.

.                                                                 1 / 1 (100%)

Time: 798 ms, Memory: 10.00Mb

OK (1 test, 1 assertion)
```

Figure 8-2. *Passed test*

So, what actually happened in our test?

```
1  public function testIfWeGetRrdAsLastRegisteredUser()
2  {
3      $actual = $this->Users->getLastRegistered();
```

The method will return a User object that will be populated from the test database.

```
4      $expected = 'rrd';
```

We define the expected value.

```
5      $this->assertEquals($expected, $actual->username);
6  }
```

And then do the assertion. If everything is fine, $actual->username should be 'rrd'.

Take your UsersFixture.php file and add a new record. If the second user's creation time was earlier than rrd's, your test will pass. If it was created at a later time, your test will fail. When you've finished playing with this, leave your code in such a way that your test passes. A failing test means something is wrong.

Our test finished in 798 ms. Tests should run fast. Always keep your eye on execution time.

Tests and Fat Models

One concept of writing better code is to have fat models and thin controllers.

This means that the controllers should be really thin, just for a translator layer between requests and responses. So, the business logic is in models that are frequently used by controllers.

Another concept is smaller is better. This means we should have small methods. There are those who advocate a maximum of three lines per method; others recommend a maximum ten lines. Short methods are easier to read, understand, maintain, and easy to test. Longer methods can easily break the single-responsibility principle.

All these together mean that we will have fat models with many short methods that are responsible for only one thing. And perhaps you are going to have tests for all your model methods.

Tests will help you to identify the bad coding patterns that you follow and cause problems for you.

CakePHP follows the Model-View-Controller (MVC) pattern, offers good support, and helps you to follow along, even if programming patterns are new to you. Let's say that we want to have a list of users grouped by the first character of their names. So, something like *A*: Amindala, *B*: Ben Kenobi, Boba Fett, etc. Perhaps we want a list of links, so that if the user clicks someone's name, he or she will be redirected to the user's profile page.

To meet this requirement, we should query our user table for the usernames, then set the result available for the view and build up an HTML list.

The communication with the database should be in our model. All your find() calls should be in models.

The controller will check users' permissions and set variables for the views to display or flash error messages.

The view should actually build up the HTML list and links. View should not do any business logic, only print out output. If you have print (or echo) statements in your controller or model, you have broken the MVC pattern. At the same time, most of the view code should be printing only output and not anything else. An exception is calculating table summaries or averages.

Test Callbacks

You may have noticed that some functions are automatically generated by bake. These are test callbacks. CakePHP's unit tests have the following callback methods:

- setUp is called before every test method, so this is the best place to put initialization of generally used objects. You should always call parent::setUp().

- tearDown is called after every test method. Don't forget to call parent::tearDown.

The tearDownAfterClass is called once, after the test methods in a case are started. This method must be static.

Summary

In this chapter, we wrote our first unit test. At first, it failed, as we followed TDD. You learned the main principle of test methods: how assertions work. You also learned about fat models and the differences between models, controllers, and views. Finally, you learned about test callbacks.

Yes, learning by trying and doing is the root of coding

CHAPTER 9

Controller Tests 1

In chapter 7, you saw that model tests extend TestCase. Controller tests extend IntegrationTestCase. Using this as base classes will simulate get, post calls, and check for response objects.

Overview of the Baked Controller

Take a look at the /src/Controllers/PostsController.php file that we generated by bake earlier.

```
1    <?php
2    namespace App\Controller;
3
```

All controllers share the same namespace, which is App\Controller.

```
4    use App\Controller\AppController;
5
```

With the use operator, we import the App\Controller\AppController namespace.

```
6    /**
7     * Posts Controller
8     *
9     * @property \App\Model\Table\PostsTable $Posts
10    */
11   class PostsController extends AppController
12   {
13
```

All controller classes extend the AppController class, which is an extension of Cake's Controller class. It ensures that we can use components and have methods for redirection, etc.

```
14      /**
15       * Index method
16       *
17       * @return \Cake\Network\Response|null
18       */
19      public function index()
20      {
```

The index method generated by bake is for listing all posts.

```
21          $this->paginate = [
22              'contain' => ['Categories', 'Users']
23          ];
24          $posts = $this->paginate($this->Posts);
25
```

We want to use pagination in our view, to allow the user to paginate, if there are many posts. We load the associated Categories and Users models to see the post's related data.

```
26          $this->set(compact('posts'));
27          $this->set('_serialize', ['posts']);
28      }
29
```

Then we set the variables for the view. We set only one variable, post, and then set the _serialize variable, as it may be useful in JSON responses.

```
30      /**
31       * View method
32       *
33       * @param string|null $id Post id.
34       * @return \Cake\Network\Response|null
35       * @throws \Cake\Datasource\Exception\RecordNotFoundException
36       *     When record not found.
37       */
```

The view method is for getting only one post, with all associated data, and to set the post variable for the view.

```
38    public function view($id = null)
39    {
40        $post = $this->Posts->get($id, [
41            'contain' => ['Categories', 'Users', 'Tags', 'Comments']
42        ]);
43
44        $this->set('post', $post);
45        $this->set('_serialize', ['post']);
46    }
47
```

The next method that is generated by bake is add. This method is for adding new posts.

```
48    /**
49     * Add method
50     *
51     * @return \Cake\Network\Response|void Redirects on successful
52     *    add, renders view otherwise.
53     */
54    public function add()
55    {
56        $post = $this->Posts->newEntity();
```

First, we create a new entity object for the new post.

```
57        if ($this->request->is('post')) {
58            $post = $this->Posts->patchEntity(
59                $post,
60                $this->request->data
61            );
```

If we already received some post data in the request, we load it to the $post entity object.

```
62        if ($this->Posts->save($post)) {
63            $this->Flash->success(__('The post has been saved.'));
64            return $this->redirect(['action' => 'index']);
65        } else {
66            $this->Flash->error(
67                __('The post not saved. Please, try again.')
68            );
69        }
70    }
```

Next, we try to save the new post and set a success or error message. If the save operation was successful, we redirect the user to the posts/index URL.

```
71          $categories = $this->Posts->Categories
72              ->find('list', ['limit' => 200]);
73          $users = $this->Posts->Users->find('list', ['limit' => 200]);
74          $tags = $this->Posts->Tags->find('list', ['limit' => 200]);
75          $this->set(compact('post', 'categories', 'users', 'tags'));
76          $this->set('_serialize', ['post']);
77      }
78
```

Then we set all the variables for the view.

The next method generated by bake is edit, for editing previously saved posts.

```
79      /**
80       * Edit method
81       *
82       * @param string|null $id Post id.
83       * @return \Cake\Network\Response|void Redirects
84       *        on successful edit, renders view otherwise.
85       * @throws \Cake\Network\Exception\NotFoundException
86       *        When record not found.
87       */
88      public function edit($id = null)
89      {
90          $post = $this->Posts->get($id, [
91              'contain' => ['Tags']
92          ]);
```

First, we get the post from the model identified by its id.

```
93          if ($this->request->is(['patch', 'post', 'put'])) {
94              $post = $this->Posts->patchEntity(
95                  $post,
96                  $this->request->data
97              );
98              if ($this->Posts->save($post)) {
99                  $this->Flash->success(__('The post has been saved.'));
100                 return $this->redirect(['action' => 'index']);
101             } else {
102                 $this->Flash->error(
103                     __('The post not saved. Please, try again.')
104                 );
105             }
106         }
```

If we receive post data in the request by HTTP patch, post, or put methods, we try to save the post.

```
107        $categories = $this->Posts->Categories
108            ->find('list', ['limit' => 200]);
109        $users = $this->Posts->Users->find('list', ['limit' => 200]);
110        $tags = $this->Posts->Tags->find('list', ['limit' => 200]);
111        $this->set(compact('post', 'categories', 'users', 'tags'));
112        $this->set('_serialize', ['post']);
113    }
114
```

Then again, as in the previous methods, we set up the variables that will be used in the corresponding view.

The last method generated by bake is delete, to remove posts already saved.

```
115    /**
116     * Delete method
117     *
118     * @param string|null $id Post id.
119     * @return \Cake\Network\Response|null Redirects to index.
120     * @throws \Cake\Datasource\Exception\RecordNotFoundException
121     *      When record not found.
122     */
123    public function delete($id = null)
124    {
125        $this->request->allowMethod(['post', 'delete']);
126        $post = $this->Posts->get($id);
127        if ($this->Posts->delete($post)) {
128            $this->Flash->success(__('The post has been deleted.'));
129        } else {
130            $this->Flash->error(
131                __('The post not deleted. Please, try again.')
132            );
133        }
134        return $this->redirect(['action' => 'index']);
135    }
136 }
```

The method is straightforward: we delete the post identified by its id and then redirect the user to posts/index.

The Magic Behind Bake

A lot of clever programming tools were used by the CakePHP team to create a handy tool like bake. As you can see in the preceding example, it really writes code for us.

When we bake models, they detect the database field types and, based on that, create entity and model classes. Entity objects represent a database row, while model objects represent a database table, with its associations, validation rules, and methods. As models extend CakePHP's Table class, they inherit a lot of useful methods. That is how we can use methods such as get, save, and delete without creating these methods. They are there as a result of the framework itself.

When we bake controllers, index, edit, view, and delete methods will be generated, as these are the most commonly used operations. These methods will use the associated models.

Baking also generates views for all the controller methods. So, for the index method, the index view is generated. In the view, we will access those variables that were set in the controller.

As you can see, by inheritance and bake, we got a lot of things out of the oven. There is, however, one thing that you should keep in your mind. Code generated by bake is just for getting a working skeleton as fast as possible. It does not handle permissions or user authentication, so anybody can create and delete things. CakePHP can provide nice support for these also, but they are not automatically generated by bake.

Creating Controller Tests

Having had an overview of the generated controller, let's create some tests for it. First, we must create fixtures for our categories, tags, and posts models. Let's start with the categories. Chapter 7 provided an overview of fixtures, so the following code sample should be clear.

```
1   <?php
2   namespace App\Test\Fixture;
3
4   use Cake\TestSuite\Fixture\TestFixture;
5
6   class CategoriesFixture extends TestFixture
7   {
8
9       public $import = ['model' => 'Categories'];
10
11      public $records = [
12          [
13              'id' => 1,
14              'category' => 'Category 1'
15          ],
```

```
16            [
17                    'id' => 2,
18                    'category' => 'Category 2'
19            ],
20        ];
21  }
```

We imported the Categories model into the fixture and created two category records. This code should be in the /tests/Fixture/CategoriesFixture.php file. The file is generated by bake. Feel free to modify it, or just create a new one with the content above.

```
1  <?php
2  namespace App\Test\Fixture;
3
4  use Cake\TestSuite\Fixture\TestFixture;
5
6  class TagsFixture extends TestFixture
7  {
8      public $import = ['model' => 'Tags'];
9
10      public $records = [
11          [
12                  'id' => 1,
13                  'tag' => 'Tag 1'
14          ],
15          [
16                  'id' => 2,
17                  'tag' => 'Tag 2'
18          ],
19          [
20                  'id' => 3,
21                  'tag' => 'Tag 3'
22          ],
23      ];
24  }
```

We should do the same for tags. In this case, we create three tags. It should go to the /tests/Fixture/TagsFixture.php file.

```
1  <?php
2  namespace App\Test\Fixture;
3
4  use Cake\TestSuite\Fixture\TestFixture;
5
6  class PostsFixture extends TestFixture
7  {
8      public $import = ['model' => 'Posts'];
9
```

```
10      public $records = [
11          [
12              'id' => 1,
13              'category_id' => 1,
14              'user_id' => 1,
15              'title' => 'First Post Tilte',
16              'body' => 'This is the body of the first post...',
17              'created' => '2016-05-01 13:00:00',
18              'modified' => '2016-05-01 13:00:00'
19          ],
20      ];
21  }
```

We should do the same for posts. Right now, one record would be enough. This code should be in the /tests/Fixture/PostsFixture.php file.

We have a belongsToMany association between posts and tags, meaning a post can have many tags, and a tag can be assigned to many posts. For storing this data, we have created a posts_tags database table in our default data source. As we want to use it now in tests, we need fixtures for our join tables also.

```
1   <?php
2   namespace App\Test\Fixture;
3
4   use Cake\TestSuite\Fixture\TestFixture;
5
6   class PostsTagsFixture extends TestFixture
7   {
8       public $import = ['model' => 'PostsTags'];
9
10      public $records = [
11          [
12              'post_id' => 1,
13              'tag_id' => 1
14          ],
15          [
16              'post_id' => 1,
17              'tag_id' => 3
18          ],
19      ];
20  }
```

You can see that the post with the id 1 has two tags, with id 1 and 3.

Now we have all the required fixtures. We already baked /tests/TestCase/Controller/PostsControllerTest.php, but, just for fun, delete it and create another one from scratch.

Our test case should have its namespace and will use PostsController and
IntegrationTestCase, so we load them.

```
1   <?php
2   namespace App\Test\TestCase\Controller;
3
4   use App\Controller\PostsController;
5   use Cake\TestSuite\IntegrationTestCase;
6
```

Let's create our base class.

```
7   class PostsControllerTest extends IntegrationTestCase
8   {
9
```

We load the fixtures into our test case.

```
10  public $fixtures = [
11        'app.posts',
12        'app.categories',
13        'app.users',
14        'app.tags',
15        'app.posts_tags'
16  ];
17
```

We do not load the comments fixture, as we do not use it in any of the tests. Loading it
would be unnecessary and would slow down test running.

And, finally, create an empty test function just to be loyal to test-driven development
(TDD).

```
18      public function testIndex()
19      {
20          $this->markTestIncomplete('Not implemented yet.');
21      }
22  }
```

The method markTestIncomplete is inherited from IntegrationTestCase and is
defined in PHPUnit. It serves a simple purpose, which is not a great surprise: it marks the
test incomplete. The actual test function requires a little more explanation, so we will add
it later.

About Integration Tests

Integration tests allow you to test your application at a higher level. It simulates an HTTP request sent to your application. Testing your controller will also use all components, models, and helpers related to the given request.

The following methods can be used for simulating HTTP requests:

- `get()` sends a GET request

- `post()` sends a POST request

- `put()` sends a PUT request

- `delete()` sends a DELETE request

- `patch()` sends a PATCH request

Assertion Methods

By using `IntegrationTestCase`, we gain access to a lot of different assertion methods. Following are some of the most useful ones:

- `$this->assertResponseOk();` checks if we got a 2xx response code on calling the controller.

- `$this->assertResponseSuccess();` checks if we got a 2xx or 3xx response code on calling the controller.

- `$this->assertResponseError();` checks if we got a 4xx response code on calling the controller.

- `$this->assertResponseFailure();` checks if we got a 5xx response code on calling the controller.

- `$this->assertResponseCode(404);` checks if the response code is 404.

- `$this->assertRedirectContains('/posts/edit/');` checks a part of the location header for redirects.

- `$this->assertResponseEquals('Call out Gouranga and be Happy!');` checks if the response content equals the given value.

- `$this->assertResponseContains('Gouranga!');` checks if the response content contains the given value.

- `$this->assertResponseNotContains('You are logged in!');` checks if the response content does not contain the given value.

- `$this->assertSession(1, 'Auth.User.id');` checks the session variable.

- $this->assertEquals('rrd', $this->viewVariable('username')); checks the view variables.

- $this->assertContentType('application/json'); checks the content types.

Setting Request Data

Most of the time, we need data in our controller, to work with what can come from get, post, cookie, or session.

```
1  public function testAdd()
2  {
3      $data = [
4          'category_id' => 2,
5          'user_id' => 1,
6          'title' => 'Test Post Title',
7          'body' => 'Test post body with same sample text',
8          'created' => '2016-05-01 14:00:00',
9          'modified' => '2016-05-01 14:00:00',
10         'tags' => [
11             ['id' => 1],
12             ['id' => 2],
13         ]
14     ];
15     $this->post('/posts/add/', $data);
16
17     $this->assertResponseSuccess();
18
```

First, we create a data array to post to the controller. Then we post it at check, if we received a success response code.

```
19     $posts = TableRegistry::get('Posts');
20     $query = $posts->find()->where(['title' => $data['title']]);
21     $this->assertEquals(1, $query->count());
22
```

In the previous chapter, we created our post's fixtures. So, we know that only this new post has the same title as the data array, so the count should return 1.

```
23     $result = $query->toArray();
24     $poststags = TableRegistry::get('PostsTags');
25     $query = $poststags->find()->where(['post_id' => $result[0]->id]);
26     $result = $query->toArray();
27     $this->assertEquals(1, $result[0]->tag_id);
28     $this->assertEquals(2, $result[1]->tag_id);
29 }
```

In the last assertion, we check if this new post has two tags, 1 and 2. (See Figure 9-1.)

```
rrd@rrd-ubuntu:~/public_html/cakeBlog$ vendor/bin/phpunit --filter testAdd tests
/TestCase/Controller/PostsControllerTest.php
PHPUnit 5.3.2 by Sebastian Bergmann and contributors.

.                                                             1 / 1 (100%)

Time: 4.36 seconds, Memory: 12.00Mb

OK (1 test, 7 assertions)
```

Figure 9-1. *Result of* testAdd

Testing GET data is really simple. You just have to add the query string into the get call's first parameter. (See Figure 9-2.)

```
rrd@rrd-ubuntu:~/public_html/cakeBlog$ vendor/bin/phpunit --filter testEdit test
s/TestCase/Controller/PostsControllerTest.php
PHPUnit 5.3.2 by Sebastian Bergmann and contributors.

.                                                             1 / 1 (100%)

Time: 4.75 seconds, Memory: 12.00Mb

OK (1 test, 4 assertions)
```

Figure 9-2. *Result of* testEdit

```
1  public function testEdit()
2  {
3      $this->get('/posts/edit/1');
4      $this->assertResponseOk();
5  }
```

Summary

This chapter provided an overview of a controller generated by bake. I discussed how bake works and what its limitations are. We then created a controller test and introduced integration testing and controller-specific assertion methods.

Little pig, little pig, let me in

CHAPTER 10

Mocks

We often require mocked components, models, objects, or even core PHP functions. You can create mocks in any of the test functions or, if you require mock objects in all of the test functions, in the setUp() method.

Mocks ensure that your tests run faster, without actually having all the required objects.

Mocking Sessions

The IntegrationTestCase class provides a few helper methods to mock request objects, including sessions, cookies, headers, etc.

Let's see an example for session variables. The others work similarly.

Create the test method first. Change your testIndex() method in the /tests/TestCase/Controller/CategoriesControllerTest.php file.

```
1  public function testIndex()
2  {
3      $this->get('/categories');
4      $this->assertResponseNotContains('Category 2');
5
6      $this->session(['isAdmin' => true]);
7      $this->get('/categories');
8      $this->assertResponseContains('Category 2');
9  }
```

We defined two assertions. Both call /categories, the first one without defining the session variable, the second with the session variable. So, the first should not contain Category 2, but the second should. The value Category 2 comes from the fixture that we created in Chapter 9.

© Sándor Gömöri 2016
S. Gömöri, *Learn CakePHP*, DOI 10.1007/978-1-4842-1212-7_10

Update your index() method in your /src/Controller/CategoriesController.php file.

```
1   public function index()
2   {
3       if (!$this->request->session()->read('isAdmin')) {
4           $this->paginate['limit'] = 1;
5       }
6       $categories = $this->paginate($this->Categories);
7       $this->set(compact('categories'));
8       $this->set('_serialize', ['categories']);
9   }
10
```

If you do not have the isAdmin session variable, limit the categories' list to 1. This example is a little silly, but it shows you how to mock session variables.

Mocking Model Methods

Sometimes, you want to mock model methods, to save time or just make things easier. In test-driven development (TDD), mocking can help you to test even when a method is not yet written. A mock can give you the required return values, so that you can work on tests while another team member is working on the method that is mocked. Let's see a few examples of how to use mocks.

Create a new test in the CategoriesTableTest.php file.

```
1   public function testDoSomething()
2   {
3       $this->assertTrue($this->Categories->doSomething());
4   }
```

Let's create the tested method itself, in the /src/Model/Table/CategoriesTable.php file.

```
1   public function doSomething()
2   {
3       if ($this->slowFunction()) {
4           return true;
5       } else {
6           return false;
7       }
8   }
9
10  public function slowFunction ()
11  {
12      sleep(30);
13      return true;
14  }
```

Again, a silly example, but it shows what we want. The doSomething() method calls another function that is really slow. If we run the test, it will be successful, but it needs more than 30 seconds to run. Definitely, we do not want to run it many times. At testDoSomething(), we want to test doSomething(), not slowFunction(). Let's mock it.

Perhaps we should test slowFunction() also, but that is another story.

```
1  public function testDoSomething ()
2  {
3      $model = $this->getMockForModel('Categories', ['slowFunction']);
4      $model->expects($this->once())
5          ->method('slowFunction')
6          ->will($this->returnValue(true));
7      $this->assertTrue($model->doSomething());
8  }
```

Let me explain what happens here.

We put the mock directly into the test method, because we need it here only; otherwise, we can put it into the setUp() method, to make it available to all tests.

Then we generate the mock object with the getMockForModel() method call. The first parameter of this method is an alias for the mocked table class. The second parameter is the array of mocked methods, in our case, only for the slowFunction() method.

Then, with the expects() call, we make sure that when the model invokes $this->slowFunction() the *first* time, it should return true. After this, we call $model->doSomething() for assertion. It will call the mocked slowFunction() method.

Expects Method

The expects method accepts the following parameter values:

- once() will pass if the method is called exactly once.

- never() will fail if the method is ever called.

- any() will pass if the method is called zero or more times.

- at($index) will match at call $index. The index value will be incremented each time a mock method is called, not just when the indicated method is called.

- exactly($times) will only pass if the method is called $times times.

- atLeastOnce() will pass if the method is called more than once.

A More Complex Mock Example

Mocks can be as simple as in the previous example or more complex, as your test requires. Keep in mind that too complex mocks will make the test less readable, so a better practice is to use simpler mocks and have more test methods to test different situations. Anyway, here is a more complex mock example:

```
1  $model = $this->getMockForModel('Categories', ['hasPostsCount']);
2  $model->expects($this->any())
3      ->method('hasPostsCount')
4      ->with($this->logicalOr(5, 10, $this->anything()))
5      ->will(
6          $this->returnCallback(
7              function ($param) {
8                  if ($param == 5) {
9                      return [5, 10, 15];
10                 } elseif ($param == 10) {
11                     return [10, 20, 30];
12                 } else {
13                     return false;
14                 }
15             }
16         )
17     );
18 $model->expects($this->any())
19     ->method('hasPostsCount')
20     ->will($this->returnValue(null));
21 $this->assertEquals([5, 10, 15],$model->hasPostsCount(5));
22 $this->assertEquals([10, 20, 30], $model->hasPostsCount(10));
23 $this->assertEquals(false, $model->hasPostsCount(1));
```

I think this example is straightforward enough. If the model calls

- hasPostsCount(5), it will return [5, 10, 15]

- hasPostsCount(10), it will return [10, 20, 30]

- hasPostsCount(any other value), it will return false.

Remember: We actually do not have the hasPostsCount() method in our Categories table class. So, with mocking, we can use methods before we even write them.

Check the PHPUnit Manual (www.phpunit.de/manual/3.0/en/api.html) for the complete list of expects methods.

Mocking Core PHP Functions

Sometimes, though rarely, we have to mock core PHP functions, for example, to test file uploads, handling streams, time and date, etc. So, it is useful when the code depends on something that we do not have with tests.

Let's look at an example. In our blog app, we want to build up a CSV import functionality with which the user can upload tags, as manually creating a lot of them can be boring.

Add the following lines to the end of your /tests/TestCase/Model/Table/ TagsTableTest.php file.

```
1  public function testProcessFile()
2  {
3      $actual = $this->Tags->processFile('noFile');
4      $this->assertTrue($actual);
5  }
```

Perhaps we should create the processFile method itself. Add the following to the /src/Model/Table/TagsTable.php file:

```
1  public function processFile($file)
2  {
3      if (is_uploaded_file($file)) {
4          //process the file
5          return true;
6      }
7      return false;
8  }
```

This method does not do anything with the file, as file processing is not part of the discussion topic now. The only interesting part is that we call the is_uploaded_file PHP core function.

Let's run the test.

vendor/bin/phpunit --filter testProcessFile tests/TestCase/Model/Table/ TagsTableTest.php

Not a great surprise. The test fails, as we did not upload anything (see Figure 10-1). And the thing is, we do not want to upload anything at all, as we want to test the file processing, not the file uploading. So, what we want is for is_uploaded_file to return true, despite the fact that we do not upload a file.

85

```
rrd@rrd-ubuntu:~/public_html/cakeBlog$ vendor/bin/phpunit --filter testProcessFi
le tests/TestCase/Model/Table/TagsTableTest.php
PHPUnit 5.3.2 by Sebastian Bergmann and contributors.

F                                                              1 / 1 (100%)

Time: 4.53 seconds, Memory: 8.00Mb

There was 1 failure:

1) App\Test\TestCase\Model\Table\TagsTableTest::testProcessFile
Failed asserting that false is true.

/home/rrd/public_html/cakeBlog/tests/TestCase/Model/Table/TagsTableTest.php:101

FAILURES!
Tests: 1, Assertions: 1, Failures: 1.  _
```

Figure 10-1. *Failed test of the core PHP function*

PHP namespaces allow us to re-declare or overwrite PHP core functions exclusively for that namespace, so that we don't pollute other parts of the code.

 The following solution is just a workaround. Having more namespaces in a single file is a bad practice.

Add the following lines to the beginning of your TagsTableTest.php file:

```
1  <?php
2  namespace {
3      // This allows us to configure the behavior of the "global mock"
4      $mockIsUploadedFile = false;
5  }
6
```

At line 4, we create a variable, $mockIsUploadedFile, for the global namespace. We use this variable to switch between the PHP core is_uploaded_file function and its corresponding redefined namespace variant.

```
7   namespace App\Model\Table {
8       function is_uploaded_file()
9       {
10          global $mockIsUploadedFile;
11          if ($mockIsUploadedFile === true) {
12              return true;
13          } else {
14              return call_user_func_array(
```

```
15                    '\is_uploaded_file',
16                    func_get_args()
17              );
18          }
19      }
20  }
```

At line 8, we re-declare the is_uploaded_file function for the \App\Model\Table namespace. If $mockIsUploadedFile is true, we just return true as a mocked result; otherwise, we call PHP's core is_uploaded_file function.

The last thing that we have to do in this file is to replace the original namespace simple declaration with a curly bracket syntax.

At line 22, we have the following simple declaration:

```
22  namespace App\Test\TestCase\Model\Table;
```

This should be changed to curly bracket declaration, as follows:

```
22  namespace App\Test\TestCase\Model\Table {
```

Perhaps this means that we should add a closing curly bracket at the end of the file—and indent everything in this namespace one level.

At this point, our test should run successfully and yield a green bar.

Summary

In this chapter, the concept of mocks was introduced. You learned how to mock session and request data and model methods. An example of mocking a core PHP function was provided, and you learned when to use it.

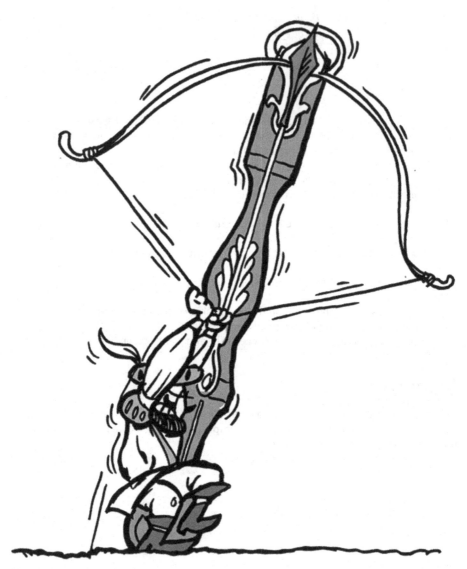

I feel some tension here

CHAPTER 11

Controller Tests 2

Testing with Authentication

There is a good chance that you will use authentication in your controllers. Authentication will not be introduced now, so I will not explain the related code in detail. In our blog, anyone can edit and delete anything, even without being logged in. Authentication is the way to let the user log in and to distinguish between logged-in and not-logged-in users. Authorization is the way to handle permissions, such that admins can edit all posts, but a user can only edit his or her own posts.

CakePHP provides nice support for handling both authentication and authorization.

At your /src/Controller/CommentsController.php file you should have the following code. In short, this code ensures that non-authenticated users cannot access any comments-related URLs, except index and add, which are accessible without authentication.

```
1   public function initialize()
2   {
3       parent::initialize();
4       $this->loadComponent(
5           'Auth',
6           [
7               'loginRedirect' => [
8                   'controller' => 'Users',
9                   'action' => 'login'
10              ]
11          ]
12      );
13  }
14
15  public function beforeFilter(Event $event)
16  {
17      parent::beforeFilter($event);
18      $this->Auth->allow(['index', 'add']);
19  }
```

© Sándor Gömöri 2016
S. Gömöri, *Learn CakePHP*, DOI 10.1007/978-1-4842-1212-7_11

Do not forget to add use Cake\Event\Event; at the beginning of this file, as we use the Event class in the beforeFilter() method.

Your browser at http://localhost/~rrd/cakeBlog/comments should show your comments, if there are any, but http://localhost/~rrd/cakeBlog/comments/view/1 should redirect you to http://localhost/~rrd/cakeBlog/users/login, as we are not logged in. We did not create login functionality yet.

Let's create a test at the /tests/TestCase/Controller/CommentsControllerTest. php file. The following test should run successfully:

```
1  public function testIndex()
2  {
3      $this->get('/comments');
4      $this->assertResponseOk();
5  }
```

Let's explore a test for a method that requires authentication. As we are not authenticated, we should be redirected to the login page. We check this by calling the assertRedirect() method.

```
1  public function testViewUnauthenticated()
2  {
3      $this->get('/comments/view/1');
4      $this->assertRedirect(
5          [
6              'controller' => 'Users',
7              'action' => 'login'
8          ]
9      );
10 }
```

You already saw how to mock the session variable, and we precisely need that here, as login data is stored in session.

```
1  public function testViewAuthenticated()
2  {
3      $this->session([
4          'Auth' => [
5              'User' => [
6                  'id' => 1,
7                  'username' => 'rrd',
8                  'role' => 10
9              ]
10         ]
11     ]);
12     $this->get('/comments/view/1');
13     $this->assertResponseOk();
14 }
```

If we are logged in, we should get an OK response and not a redirect.

Testing JSON Response

JSON (JavaScript Object Notation) is a standard format that uses human-readable text to transmit data objects consisting of attribute-value pairs. JSON is a language-independent data format. Originally, it was created for JavaScript, but to generate and parse JSON-format data, is available in many programming languages. The JSON file name extension is .json.

Here is a sample JSON string:

```
{
  "name": "rrd",
  "isAlive": true,
  "age": 40,
  "phoneNumbers": [
    {
      "type": "home",
      "number": "987 654 3210"
    },
    {
      "type": "mobile",
      "number": "123 456 7890"
    }
  ],
  "children": [],
  "spouse": "syj"
}
```

A real sample JSON file can be found in your root directory, as composer puts its composer.json there.

Webservices' Ajax call responses are in JSON or in XML. To test these responses, we should first add the RequestHandler component to our controller's initialize() method, as follows.

```
1   $this->loadComponent('RequestHandler');
```

We should add the following line to the /config/routes.php file around line 45, to let it handle the json extension.

```
1   Router::extensions(['json']);
```

Let's create our test method in the CommentsControllerTest.php file.

```
1  public function testAdd()
2  {
3      $this->configRequest(
4          [
5              'headers' => ['Accept' => 'application/json']
6          ]
7      );
8      $data = [
9          'comment' => 'Call out Gouranga and be happy',
10         'user_id' => 1,
11         'post_id' => 1,
12         'category_id' => 2
13     ];
14     $this->post('/comments/add.json', $data);
15     $this->assertResponseSuccess();
16
17     $expected = [
18         'comment' => [
19             'comment' => 'Call out Gouranga and be happy',
20             'user_id' => 1,
21             'post_id' => 1,
22             'category_id' => 2,
23             'id' => 2
24         ],
25     ];
26     $expected = json_encode($expected, JSON_PRETTY_PRINT);
27     $this->assertEquals($expected, $this->_response->body());
28 }
```

First, we mock the headers, then the post data, and then check the response HTTP header code and its content.

In your CommentsController.php file's add() method, remove (or comment out) the following line:

```
1  return $this->redirect(['action' => 'index']);
```

You should have something like the following:

```
1  public function add()
2  {
3      $comment = $this->Comments->newEntity();
4      if ($this->request->is('post')) {
5          $comment = $this->Comments->patchEntity(
6              $comment,
7              $this->request->data
8          );
```

```
9          if ($this->Comments->save($comment)) {
10             $this->Flash->success(__('The comment has been saved.'));
11             //return $this->redirect(['action' => 'index']);
12         } else {
13             $this->Flash->error(
14                 __('The comment not saved. Please, try again.')
15             );
16         }
17     }
18     $users = $this->Comments->Users->find('list', ['limit' => 200]);
19     $posts = $this->Comments->Posts->find('list', ['limit' => 200]);
20     $this->set(compact('comment', 'users', 'posts'));
21     $this->set('_serialize', ['comment']);
22 }
```

Now our test should run successfully.

Summary

In this chapter, you learned how to test the functionality behind authentication by mocking. Then you saw an example of testing controllers that respond to JSON data in spite of HTML.

This suit really suits me

CHAPTER 12

Test Suites

While developing a particular feature, we'll run certain tests. Before deploying, we should run all our tests, to make sure we haven't broken something. This is the point at which test suites come into the picture.

Using TestSuite

TestSuite offers a few methods for easily creating test suites, based on the file system.

To create a test suite for *all* model table tests, we should create a file named AllModelTableTest.php in /tests/TestCase/.

```php
1   <?php
2   use Cake\TestSuite\TestSuite;
3
4   class AllModelTableTest extends TestSuite
5   {
6       public static function suite() {
7           $suite = new TestSuite('All model table tests');
8           $suite->addTestDirectory(TESTS . 'TestCase/Model/Table');
9           return $suite;
10      }
11  }
12
```

The preceding code groups all test cases found in the /tests/TestCase/Model/ Table folder.

Now you can run all your model table tests at once.

```
$ cd ~/public_html/cakeBlog
$ vendor/bin/phpunit tests/TestCase/AllModelTableTest.php
```

You can create a test suite for all controllers, etc., in the same way.

If you want to add only a few files, you can use $suite->addTestFile($filename).

You can add directories recursively under /tests/TestCase by $suite->addTestDi rectoryRecursive(TESTS . 'TestCase');, so you can run all your tests at once. Do not forget that simply using vendor/bin/phpunit does the same.

Using phpunit.xml

The other option to create test suites is to add them into a /phpunit.xml.dist file. This file was automatically created when we installed cakephp via composer. By default, PHPUnit will look for a file named either phpunit.xml or phpunit.xml.dist in the directory in which you run it, and it will use the values it contains to alter its own behavior. In the case of CakePHP, this file is in the root directory of our app.

This XML file describes different settings for our tests. There is a <testsuites> section wherein you can define new test suites. Let's add the following lines as a new child element of the <testsuites> element.

```
1  <testsuite name="ExcitingFeature">
2      <directory>src/Model/Table</directory>
3      <exclude>src/Model/Table/CommentsTableTest.php</exclude>
4      <file>tests/TestCase/Controller/CommentsControllerTest.php</file>
5  </testsuite>
```

Our new test suite's name is ExcitingFeature, because we group those tests that are related to a new feature in what we are working on.

There can be multiple <directory> elements. PHPUnit will add all tests in that directory recursively.

There can be multiple <exclude> elements. This is not a great surprise, but these files will be excluded.

There can be multiple <file> elements also. These files will be added to the test suite.

Summary

I dedicated this short chapter to testing suites. You learned how to group certain tests, by using the TestSuite object or the phpunit.xml file.

You need the right tools to do good work

CHAPTER 13

Testing from Command Line

Running tests can be time-consuming, but this doesn't require any user interaction. For that reason, tests are ideal targets for automation. CakePHP has a built-in test shell that we've already used in the previous chapters. As was mentioned earlier, testing in the browser is boring, time-consuming, and not the best option. With unit tests, you can develop without touching the browser. This one thing can significantly shorten development time.

Debug Messages

Debug messages are written into the console, so you can see them by executing your tests. So, if you have debug($result); in your code, the output of this call will be available at the console.

Run All Tests

Before deployment, you are going to run all tests, to check that all is correct. The following command will run all your tests:

```
$ cd ~/public_html/cakeBlog
$ vendor/bin/phpunit
```

A middle-size project with good test coverage can take from thirty minutes to two to three hours to run.

Run Test Suites

The next level is to run test suites. This is required when you are working on a feature and have a test suite for that feature.

© Sándor Gömöri 2016
S. Gömöri, *Learn CakePHP*, DOI 10.1007/978-1-4842-1212-7_13

If you used TestSuite, then you are going to run something such as the following:

```
$ cd ~/public_html/cakeBlog
$ vendor/bin/phpunit tests/TestCase/AllModelTableTest.php
```

If you defined your test suite in phpunit.xml.dist, you need the following command:

```
$ cd ~/public_html/cakeBlog
$ vendor/bin/phpunit --testsuite ExcitingFeature
```

Run All Tests in a File

When you want to run all tests in a test file, for example, in your UsersTableTest.php file, you should run the following command:

```
$ cd ~/public_html/cakeBlog
$ vendor/bin/phpunit tests/TestCase/Model/Table/UsersTableTest.php
```

You will use this when you work only on one model. Your models are loosely coupled, so you only want to check one model.

Filtering Test Cases

During development, most of the time, you are going to run only one test on what you are currently working on. The --filter option serves this purpose.

```
$ cd ~/public_html/cakeBlog
$ vendor/bin/phpunit --filter testDoSomething tests/TestCase/Model/Table/
CategoriesTableTest.php
```

Understanding a Failing Test's Output

PHPUnit shows the differences between the actual and expected results on assertions.

We have already created /tests/Fixture/CommentsFixture.php, so this is the time to change the $records array.

```
1  public $records = [
2      [
3          'id' => 1,
4          'comment' => 'This is my first comment.',
5          'user_id' => 1,
6          'post_id' => 1
```

```
 7      ],
 8      [
 9          'id' => 2,
10          'comment' => 'This is an other comment by someone else.',
11          'user_id' => 2,
12          'post_id' => 1
13      ],
14      [
15          'id' => 3,
16          'comment' => 'Call out Gouranga and be happy',
17          'user_id' => 1,
18          'post_id' => 1
19      ],
20  ];
```

So, we have three comments, all of them belonging to the first post. Comments 1 and 3 are created by user 1; comment 2 is created by user 2.

Add a new test function to /tests/TestCase/Model/Table/CommentsTableTest. php, as follows:

```
 1  public function testGetCommentsOfUser()
 2  {
 3      $actual = $this->Comments->getCommentsOfUser(2);
 4      $expected = [
 5          [
 6              'id' => 5,
 7              'comment' => 'This is an other comment by someone else.',
 8              'user_id' => 2,
 9              'post_id' => 2
10          ]
11      ];
12      $this->assertEquals(
13          $expected,
14          $actual->hydrate(false)->toArray()
15      );
16  }
```

We expect to get the preceding array when we call getCommentsOfUser() method.

And, finally, create the getCommentsOfUser() method in /src/Model/Table/ CommentsTable.php.

```
 1  public function getCommentsOfUser($userId)
 2  {
 3      return $this->find()
 4          ->where(['user_id' => $userId]);
 5  }
```

It's now time to test.

```
$ cd ~/public_html/cakeBlog
$ vendor/bin/phpunit --filter testGetCommentsOfUser tests/TestCase/Model/
Table/CommentsTableTest.php
```

We will get the following output, shown in Figure 13-1:

```
rrd@rrd-ubuntu:~/public_html/cakeBlog$ vendor/bin/phpunit --filter testGetCommen
tsOfUser tests/TestCase/Model/Table/CommentsTableTest.php
PHPUnit 5.3.2 by Sebastian Bergmann and contributors.

█                                                              1 / 1 (100%)

Time: 1.62 seconds, Memory: 10.00Mb

There was 1 failure:

1) App\Test\TestCase\Model\Table\CommentsTableTest::testGetCommentsOfUser
Failed asserting that two arrays are equal.
--- Expected
+++ Actual
@@ @@
 Array (
     0 => Array (
-        'id' => 5
+        'id' => 2
         'comment' => 'This is an other comment by s... else.'
         'user_id' => 2
-        'post_id' => 2
+        'post_id' => 1
     )
 )

/home/rrd/public_html/cakeBlog/tests/TestCase/Model/Table/CommentsTableTest.php:
65

FAILURES!
Tests: 1, Assertions: 1, Failures: 1.
rrd@rrd-ubuntu:~/public_html/cakeBlog$ █
```

Figure 13-1. *Failing test*

The red *F* indicates that our test failed.

The next line shows the test's execution time and the memory used.

We can see which method of which test file failed, and a message describing the reason for the failure.

Then we can see the difference between the expected and the actual result. The - sign indicates the expected result; the + sign shows the actual result.

So, the figure shows that we expected an array that has only one member, which is another array. This is OK.

The expected id is 5, but the actual id is 2. The comment and user_id are equal both in expected and actual arrays, but post_id again differs.

Then the next line shows the line number of the failed assertion.

At the end, we can see the summarized report of the run tests.

Interrupting Tests

You can stop running a test at any time at the console, by pressing Ctrl+C. If you do so, do not forget to check your test database, as database entries can remain there, as you interrupt test execution before it removes all entries.

Summary

In this chapter, you learned how to use information provided by debug, how to run all tests at once, and how to filter tests. An overview of the test output was provided, and you learned how to interrupt tests.

There are other yummies

CHAPTER 14

Goodies

Code Coverage

Code coverage helps you to identify code parts that are not covered by tests. Theoretically, 100% coverage is attainable, but most of the time, you will achieve less than that percentage.

Generating code coverage is simple, like a piece of cake. We can generate coverage for all tests, test suites, or only for test files, with the same options described in the previous chapter.

```
$ cd ~/public_html/cakeBlog
$ vendor/bin/phpunit --coverage-html webroot/coverage tests/TestCase/Model/
Table/UsersTableTest.php
```

Now, open your browser and check your app's `coverage/index.html` file. In my case, this is `http://localhost/~rrd/cakeBlog/coverage/index.html` (Figure 14-1).

/home/rrd/public_html/cakeBlog/src / (Dashboard)

	Code Coverage					
	Lines		Functions and Methods		Classes and Traits	
Total	0.31%	2 / 635	0.00%	0 / 58	26.09%	6 / 23
Console	0.00%	0 / 98	0.00%	0 / 6	0.00%	0 / 1
Controller	0.00%	0 / 345	0.00%	0 / 30	0.00%	0 / 7
Model	1.32%	2 / 151	0.00%	0 / 18	50.00%	6 / 12
Shell	0.00%	0 / 35	0.00%	0 / 2	0.00%	0 / 1
View	0.00%	0 / 6	0.00%	0 / 2	0.00%	0 / 2

Legend

Low: 0% to 50%   Medium: 50% to 90%   High: 90% to 100%

Generated by PHP_CodeCoverage 3.3.1 using PHP 7.0.6-6+donate.sury.org~wily+1 and PHPUnit 5.3.2 at Wed May 11 19:12:28 UTC 2016.

Figure 14-1. *Code Coverage index page*

© Sándor Gömöri 2016
S. Gömöri, *Learn CakePHP*, DOI 10.1007/978-1-4842-1212-7_14

You can see a summary of your code coverage. As we generated only for one model file, our coverage is very low. You can click Model to view its details. We can see that only TagsTable.php has tests (Figure 14-2).

/home/rrd/public_html/cakeBlog/src / Model / Table / (Dashboard)

	Code Coverage							
	Lines		Functions and Methods			Classes and Traits		
Total	1.32%	2 / 151		0.00%	0 / 18		0.00%	0 / 6
CategoriesTable.php	0.00%	0 / 28		0.00%	0 / 4		0.00%	0 / 1
CommentsTable.php	0.00%	0 / 31		0.00%	0 / 4		0.00%	0 / 1
PostsTable.php	0.00%	0 / 38		0.00%	0 / 3		0.00%	0 / 1
PostsTagsTable.php	0.00%	0 / 17		0.00%	0 / 2		0.00%	0 / 1
TagsTable.php	66.67%	2 / 3		0.00%	0 / 1		0.00%	0 / 1
UsersTable.php	0.00%	0 / 34		0.00%	0 / 4		0.00%	0 / 1

Legend

Low: 0% to 50%   Medium: 50% to 90%   High: 90% to 100%

Generated by PHP_CodeCoverage 3.3.1 using PHP 7.0.6-6+donate.sury.org~wily+1 and PHPUnit 5.3.2 at Wed May 11 19:12:28 UTC 2016.

Figure 14-2. *Code coverage for the models*

Click this to go deeper. At the top of the page, we can see what methods we have, which of them is covered by tests, and how many lines are covered by tests (Figure 14-3).

/home/rrd/public_html/cakeBlog/src / Model / Table / TagsTable.php

	Code Coverage							
	Classes and Traits		Functions and Methods				Lines	
Total	0.00%	0 / 1		0.00%	0 / 1	CRAP	66.67%	2 / 3
TagsTable	0.00%	0 / 1		66.67%	2 / 3	4.59	66.67%	2 / 3
initialize				100.00%	1 / 1	1	100.00%	0 / 0
validationDefault				100.00%	1 / 1	1	100.00%	0 / 0
processFile				0.00%	0 / 1	2.15	66.67%	2 / 3

Figure 14-3. *Code coverage for our Tags model*

If we scroll down, we can see that the processFile() method is partially covered (Figure 14-4).

```
56
57    public function processFile($file)
58    {
59        if (is_uploaded_file($file)) {
60            //process the file
61            return true;
62        }
63        return false;
64    }
```

Figure 14-4. *Method code coverage*

Green lines are covered, red lines are not covered, and white lines are not executable.

Fixtures Data

Creating fixtures is boring, and automatically generated fixtures are filled with useless data. We need an easy, and intelligent, solution that can hold table relations with real data.

PHPMyAdmin (http://phpmyadmin.net) gives us a way to export table data. Choose PHP array as the format and custom for the type. Then you can define how many rows you want to take from your existing records.

While PHPMyAdmin is a complete MySQL administration tool with which you can create, edit, and remove databases, tables, fields, and records, it is not only for exporting data for fixtures. If you are not familiar with it, it is time to become so. If you've made friends with the Terminal, you can learn to use the MySQL console also.

Testing Private Methods

We've seen a lot of examples of testing public methods. Testing protected methods is the same.

If we try to test a private method, we will get an error message complaining about an unknown method.

Let's create a private method in /src/Model/Table/PostsTable.php:

```
1  private function getPostsInCategory($categoryId)
2  {
3      return $this->find()
4          ->where(['category_id' => $categoryId]);
5  }
```

While, again, this is a silly example of a private method, it's good enough for testing private methods.

Private methods should be instanced as a reflection class, to enable testing. Paste the following into /tests/TestCase/Model/Table/PostsTableTest.php:

```
1  public function testGetPostsInCategory()
2  {
3      $class = new ReflectionClass($this->Posts);
4      $method = $class->getMethod('getPostsInCategory');
5      $method->setAccessible(true);
6      $actual = $method->invoke($this->Posts, 1);
7      $expected = 1;
8      $this->assertEquals($expected, $actual->toArray()[0]->id);
9  }
```

To get it to work, we should include ReflectionClass at the beginning of this file.

```
1  use ReflectionClass;
```

Many developers say you shouldn't test private methods. Instead of getting into the details of their arguments, I'll leave it up to you to decide whether or not to test them.

Testing Views

Generally, we do not test views, as we do with models and controllers. HTML tends to change, and most of it is not testable. The best approach is to rely on assertContains, if you want to check data in the view. Selenium (http://seleniumhq.org/) is a tool for testing views.

Testing Components

If you created your own component at /src/Controller/Component/YourComponent.php, you should put its test file to /tests/TestCase/Controller/Component/ YourComponentTest.php.

At the setUp() method of your test class, you should mock Cake's Controller class and register your component.

A sample setUp() method is the following:

```
1  public function setUp()
2  {
3      parent::setUp();
4      $request = new Request();
5      $response = new Response();
6      $this->controller = $this->getMock(
7          'Cake\Controller\Controller',
8          null,
9          [$request, $response]
10     );
11     $registry = new ComponentRegistry($this->controller);
12     $this->component = new YourComponent($registry);
13 }
```

At the tearDown() method, we should unset the class variables created by setup().

```
1  public function tearDown()
2  {
3      parent::tearDown();
4      unset($this->component, $this->controller);
5  }
```

Let's say YourComponent manipulates pagination. It has a textToNumber() method that sets the pagination's limit to different numbers, based on textual parameters. For example, if textToNumber('long') is called, the pagination's limit will be set to 100. In this case, our test method will look like the following:

```
1  public function testTextToNumberLong()
2  {
3      $this->component->textToNumber('long');
4      $this->assertEquals(100, $this->controller->paginate['limit']);
5  }
```

We called the component's textToNumber() method and then we checked the controller's pagination limit value by the assertion.

Testing Helpers

Let's say we have a helper that creates a date string based on a given number of days passed since the millennium. Paste the following code to /src/View/Helper/EasyDateHelper.php:

```
1  namespace App\View\Helper;
2
3  use Cake\View\Helper;
4
5  class EasyDateHelper extends Helper
6  {
7      public function add($days)
8      {
9          return 'D: ' . date('Y-m-d', mktime(0, 0, 0, 1, $days, 2000));
10      }
11  }
```

The corresponding test file should be /tests/TestCase/View/Helper/EasyDateHelperTest.php. It is very similar to model tests, except we should call the helper's constructor in the setUp() method.

```
1  namespace App\Test\TestCase\View\Helper;
2
3  use App\View\Helper\EasyDateHelper;
4  use Cake\TestSuite\TestCase;
5  use Cake\View\View;
6
7  class EasyDateHelperTest extends TestCase
8  {
9
10     public $helper = null;
11
```

```
12    public function setUp()
13    {
14        parent::setUp();
15        $View = new View();
16        $this->helper = new EasyDateHelper($View);
17    }
18
19    public function testAdd()
20    {
21        $this->assertEquals('D: 2000-01-15', $this->helper->add(15));
22        $this->assertEquals('D: 2000-04-09', $this->helper->add(100));
23        $this->assertEquals('D: 2002-09-26', $this->helper->add(1000));
24    }
25  }
```

When you are testing a Helper that uses other helpers, be sure to mock the View class's loadHelpers method.

Testing Plugins

If you have a plugin called Pizza at /src/plugins, you should have all your tests in the /src/plugins/Pizza/tests folder, with the same subfolders as in /tests.

```
1  namespace Pizza\Test\TestCase\Model\Table;
2
3  use Pizza\Model\Table\PizzaSlicesTable;
4  use Cake\TestSuite\TestCase;
5
6  class PizzaSlicesTableTest extends TestCase
7  {
8      public $fixtures = ['plugin.pizza.pizza_slices'];
9
10      public function testTaste()
11      {
12          // Test taste of the pizza slices
13      }
14  }
```

Summary

In this chapter, you sampled a few goodies. First, you saw how code coverage can be generated and used, then you discovered an easy way to generate fixtures. You also learned how to test private methods, views, components, helpers, and plugins.

This is the end of my book on CakePHP and unit testing. I hope that you can use much of the information in this book and that it will help you to become a better web developer.

References by Chapter

What Is Unit Testing?

Contrarian Software Development
www.contrariansoftware.com/2008/11/unit-testing-sucks.html

IPL
www.ipl.com/pdf/p0828.pdf

Petri Kainulainen
www.petrikainulainen.net/programming/unit-testing/wrong-reasons-not-to-write-unit-tests/

Weblabor
http://weblabor.hu/cikkek/php-osztalyok-egysegtesztelese

Zen and the Art of TDD
http://vimeo.com/49092644

Clean Code

Clean Code Handbook Software Craftsmanship
www.amazon.com/Clean-Code-Handbook-Software-Craftsmanship/dp/0132350882

Test-Driven Development

Net tuts+
http://net.tutsplus.com/sessions/test-driven-php/

TDD
www.youtube.com/watch?v=fkrpMLzxWOo

© Sándor Gömöri 2016
S. Gömöri, *Learn CakePHP*, DOI 10.1007/978-1-4842-1212-7

Development Cycle

Software Development Process
http://en.wikipedia.org/wiki/Software_development_process

Others

Webmania
http://webmania.cc

Cakephp PHPUnit Testing
www.youtube.com/watch?v=L-lLSi4lXEY

Mark Story
http://mark-story.com/posts/view/getting-familiar-
with-phpunit-mocks

Index

A

Arguments, 9–11, 13, 16, 21, 108
Assertions, 20, 35, 47, 61–62, 64, 76–78,
    81, 83, 100, 102, 109
Authentication, 19, 72, 89–90, 93

B

Baking, 24, 44–45, 72
Bugfix, 13

C

Callbacks, 63–64
Command line, 99–103
Components, 68, 76, 81, 91, 108–110
Composer, 30, 32–34, 47, 91, 96
Conventions, 4–6, 16
Coverage, 99, 105–106, 110
CRUD, 4

D

Database, 4–5, 16, 24, 30, 33–47, 49, 51,
    53–54, 57, 62–63, 72, 74, 103, 107
Debug, 35, 99, 103
Design, 9, 24, 30

E

Error messages, 33, 35, 44–45, 61, 63,
    70, 107
Expects, 11, 20, 49, 60–62, 83–84, 92,
    100–102, 107

F

Failed test, 60, 86
Failing tests, 12, 61–62, 100–102
Fat model, 58, 60, 63–64
Filtering, 35, 60, 85, 90, 100, 102–103
Fixtures, 44–47, 49–57, 59, 61–62, 72–75,
    77, 81, 100, 107, 110

G

Get, 5, 12, 20, 29–32, 34, 42, 53–54, 60–62,
    69–71, 76–78, 81, 83–84, 87, 90,
    101–102, 107–108, 112

H

http requests, 76

I

Installation, 4, 29, 31–32, 34
Integration tests, 67, 75–76, 78, 81
Isolation, 9, 12, 17, 49

J, K, L

JSON, 32, 34, 68, 77, 91–93

M

Maintainable, 3, 9, 12, 15
Mess detector, 16
Mocks, 81–87, 90, 92–93, 108, 110, 112
Model-view-controller (MVC), 5, 16, 24,
    42, 44, 63

© Sándor Gömöri 2016
S. Gömöri, *Learn CakePHP*, DOI 10.1007/978-1-4842-1212-7

■ N, O

Naming, 16–17

■ P

PHP standards recommendations (PSR), 16
PHPUnit, 6, 19, 21, 29, 33–34, 47,
　　　60–61, 75, 84–85, 95–96,
　　　99–100, 102, 105, 112
phpunit.xml, 96, 100
Planning, 17, 23, 25, 37, 41–42
Post, 4–5, 15, 31–32, 37, 39–44, 46–47, 49,
　　　56, 67–78, 84, 89, 92–93, 100–102,
　　　107, 112
Private methods, 107–108, 110
PSR. *See* PHP standards
　　　recommendations (PSR)

■ Q

Quality code, 11–12

■ R

Refactoring, 10–13, 15–17, 19–21
Request, 29, 44, 62–63, 69–71, 76–78,
　　　81–82, 87, 91–92, 108
Response, 23, 44, 63, 67–71, 76–78, 81,
　　　90–93, 108

■ S

Save time, 10, 13, 82
Services, 32
Session, 42, 45–47, 76–77, 81–82, 87, 90, 111

■ T, U

Test-driven development (TDD), 9, 17,
　　　19–21, 25, 59, 61, 64, 75, 82, 111
Test groups, 95

■ V, W, X, Y, Z

Validation, 5, 72

Get the eBook for only $5!

Why limit yourself?

Now you can take the weightless companion with you wherever you go and access your content on your PC, phone, tablet, or reader.

Since you've purchased this print book, we're happy to offer you the eBook in all 3 formats for just $5.

Convenient and fully searchable, the PDF version enables you to easily find and copy code—or perform examples by quickly toggling between instructions and applications. The MOBI format is ideal for your Kindle, while the ePUB can be utilized on a variety of mobile devices.

To learn more, go to www.apress.com/companion or contact support@apress.com.

Printed in the United States
By Bookmasters